DON TROIANI'S CIVIL WAR
Zouaves, Chasseurs, Special Branches & Officers

Art by Don Troiani
Text by Earl J. Coates, Michael J. McAfee, and Don Troiani

STACKPOLE
BOOKS

David H. Madsen, PhD

Published in paperback in 2006 by
STACKPOLE BOOKS
5067 Ritter Road
Mechanicsburg, PA 17055
www.stackpolebooks.com

Printed in China

10 9 8 7 6 5 4 3 2 1

FIRST EDITION

For free information about the artwork and limited edition prints of Don Troiani, contact:

Historical Art Prints
P.O. Box 660
Southbury, CT 06488
203-262-6560
www.historicalartprints.com

For information on licensing images in this book, visit www.historicalimagebank.com

Library of Congress Cataloging-in-Publication Data

Troiani, Don.
    [Don Troiani's regiments and uniforms of the Civil War. Selections]
    Don Troiani's Civil War zouaves, chasseurs, special branches, and officers / art by Don Troiani ;
text by Earl J. Coates, Michael J. Mcafee, and Don Troiani.— 1st ed.
            p. cm.
    Reprints a section of the author's Don Troiani's regiments and uniforms of the Civil War.
Mechanicsburg, PA : Stackpole Books, c2002.
    ISBN-13: 978-0-8117-3320-5
    ISBN-10: 0-8117-3320-3
    1. United States. Army—History—Civil War, 1861–1865—Pictorial works. 2. Confederate
States of America. Army—Pictorial works. 3. Soldiers—United States—History—19th century—
Pictorial works. 4. Soldiers—Confederate States of America—Pictorial works. 5. United States.
Army—Officers—Uniforms—History—19th century—Pictorial works. 6. Confederate States of
America. Army—Officers—Uniforms—Pictorial works. 7. United States. Army—Uniforms—
History—19th century—Pictorial works. 8. Confederate States of America. Army—Uniforms—
Pictorial works. 9. United States—History—Civil War, 1861–1865—Regimental histories.
10. United States—History—Civil War, 1861–1865—Pictorial works. I. Title: Civil War zouaves,
chasseurs, special branches, and officers. II. Coates, Earl J. III. McAfee, Michael J. IV. Title.

E492.7.T765 2006
973.7'8—dc22

                                                                    2005027476

INTRODUCTION

THIS BOOK AND THE OTHERS IN THIS SERIES ARE taken from the larger volume *Don Troiani's Regiments and Uniforms of the Civil War* to provide a less expensive reference source for those interested in specific areas of Civil War uniforms. The subject of Civil War Zouave and chasseur uniforms could not be comprehensively covered in a small volume such as this, but this publication will provide a good overview.

The French-inspired clothing worn by both sides during the conflict provided possibly the most colorful aspect of the war. Sadly, it also provided a good target in some cases. The widely held belief that Zouave uniforms were totally dispensed with after the first campaigns of the war is untrue. Not only were new regiments formed, but units in regulation Federal uniform were reclothed as Zouaves as late as 1864. A number of original garments still survive, as do period photographs, clothing returns, and descriptions, all tools which were relied upon to recreate the flamboyant soldiers illustrated here.

My longtime friends, Earl J. Coates and Michael J. McAfee, represent the pinnacle of their fields in research, and working with them has always been an enjoyable and enriching experience. Contributing authors Tom Arliskis and David M. Sullivan, also leaders in their areas of study, presented fresh information and ideas. Working with primary source materials, period photography, and original artifacts gave us the opportunity to explore the dress of many units from a multi-dimensional perspective. Equally important was the wise counsel offered by some of the great Civil War collectors and students of material culture: James C. Frasca, John Henry Kurtz, Paul Loane, Dean Nelson, Michael O'Donnell, and John Ockerbloom, among many others. Their decades of practical hands-on experience provided knowledge that cannot be "book learned."

Posing fully dressed models for all the studies in the book also opened the vista of seeing what some of this stuff really looked like on the soldier. Reading about it is one thing; seeing it is quite another.

As the main topic is uniforms, we have not explored firearms or edged weapons as they are exhaustively covered by many other books. We have touched on accoutrements but not in anything approaching complete coverage, selecting mostly items that augmented illustrated uniforms.

In researching the figure studies, the authors consulted every available source. Despite our more than a hundred years of combined study, we recognize that there's a good chance that another interesting nugget of new or conflicting data, perhaps from an unpublished account or collection, could surface after this book's publication. But that is the way of historical research and, indeed, one of the facets that makes it both frustrating and fascinating. To those who are disappointed that a favorite regiment has been left out, please forgive me, I'll try to get to it in the future!

Don Troiani
Southbury, Connecticut

ACKNOWLEDGMENTS

I DEDICATE THIS BOOK TO MY FATHER, DOMINICK H. Troiani (1916–2005), 258th Field Artillery, HQ Company, 95th Infantry Division, who served his country in France and Germany in 1944–45. His war stories got me interested in all this as a child. I also dedicate it to all the gallant servicemen and women who continue to defend our country on a daily basis.

I owe a debt of gratitude to my distinguished friends Earl J. Coates and Michael J. McAfee, two of the greatest gurus on the subject of Civil War uniforms, who graciously tolerated all my ceaseless questions and, as always, shared the fruits of a lifetime research with me. They are genuinely "national treasures." Particular thanks to contributing authors Tom Arliskis, who provided important primary information on Western units, and David Sullivan renowned authority on Civil War marines.

Special credit to renowned Civil War author-photographer Michael O'Donnell for taking many of the fine color photos of artifacts for this book, and to Tracy Studios of Southbury, Connecticut.

The following individuals and institutions also contributed to the creation of this book: Gil Barrett, Bruce Bazelon, Carl Borick, Robert Braun, William Brayton, Major William Brown, William L. Brown III, Christopher Bryant, Rene Chartrand, Charles Childs, Dr. Michael Cunningham, Ray Darida, Dr. David Evans, William Erquitt, Robin Ferit, James C. Frasca, Joseph Fulginiti, Fred Gaede, Holly Hageman, Charles Harris, Randy Hackenburg, Gary Hendershott, Bruce Hermann, Steven Hill, Robert Hodge, Mark Jaeger, Les Jensen, James L. Kochan, Robert K. Krick, Michael Kramer, John Henry Kurtz, John P. Langellier, William Lazenby, Claude Levet, Paul C. Loane, Edward McGee, Bob McDonald, Steven McKinney, Howard M. Madaus, Michael P. Musick, Dean Nelson, Donna O'Brien, John Ockerbloom, Stephen Osmun, Col. J. Craig Nannos, Dean Nelson, Larry Page, Andrew Pells, Ron Palm, Nicholas Picerno, the late Brian Pohanka, Cricket Pohanka, Kenneth Powers, Shannon Pritchard, Pat Ricci, Steven Rogers, Nancy Dearing Rossbacher, A. H. Seibel Jr., Mark Sherman, Sam Small, Wes Small, James R. H. Spears, Steve Sylvia, Brendan Synonmon, William Synonmon, David Sullivan, Donald Tharpe, Mike Thorson, Warren Tice, Ken Turner, William A. Turner, Cole Unson, James Vance, Michael Vice, Gary Wilkensen, Don Williams, and Michael J. Winey.

The Booth Museum of Western Art, Cartersville, Georgia; Confederate Memorial Hall, New Orleans; Charleston Museum, Charleston, South Carolina; Connecticut Historical Society; Connecticut State Library; New York State Collection; Pamplin Historical Park and the National Museum of the Civil War Soldier; Middlesex County Historical Society; The Company of Military Historians; the Nelsonian Institute; *North South Trader* magazine; The Horse Soldier; The Union Drummer Boy; and the West Point Museum, United States Military Academy.

Zouaves and Chasseurs

THE MOST EXOTIC AND COLORFUL OF ALL THE uniforms worn during the American Civil War were those derived from the French Zouave regiments. Uniforms of chasseurs, cousins to the Zouaves, were not as elaborate but just as distinctive. Together they were an expression of the Gallic influence of Napoleon III's ill-fated second empire. France's military machine appeared to be a formidable force in the 1850s, as it came out of successful campaigns in the Crimean War and the war with Austria in 1859. American officers, including George B. McClellan, who served as military observers with the French armies became proponents of the French systems. The influences of their observations were manifested in many forms. Just prior to the war's start, the U.S. Army replaced Winfield Scott's venerable drill manual with Hardee's *Tactics*, a revised French manual for light infantry drill and formations. During the war, Federal quartermasters issued leggings and shelter tents modeled after the French originals. And soldiers of both the North and the South wore homegrown versions of the French Zouave and chasseur uniforms.

In 1861, there were three regiments of Zouaves in the French Army. Their origins went back to 1830, when many of the French expeditionary troops were withdrawn from North Africa, and General Clausel recruited native North African troops as replacements. Among them were the *Zoudaouas,* the former ruling dey's militia, who offered their

services to the French general. He accepted, and thus were born the legendary Zouaves. In 1831, King Louis-Philippe officially sanctioned the Zouave Corps as part of the French colonial forces. By 1835, there were two battalions of six companies in the corps. Two companies of each battalion were composed of French citizens at this time, but by 1841, only one company of nine was of native North African soldiers. By 1852, the three battalions were all European (the native troops were now in sharpshooter battalions known as the *Tirailleurs Algériens*), and the original battalions became the three regiments of Frenchmen now known as Zouaves.

Despite the Europeanization of the Zouaves, their uniforms remained that of the native North African. By the time of the American Civil War, they were well established, if not indeed traditional. The Zouave was distinguished by his

These once luxurious and expensive red velvet shoulder straps are of the type labeled "extra rich" in a Schuyler, Hartley & Graham military goods catalog. No artillery colonel wore these straps, however, for they belonged to Gouverneur Kemble Warren and were worn by him while commanding the famous Duryée Zouaves, the 5th New York Volunteer Infantry. WEST POINT MUSEUM.

1

short, dark blue jacket, worn open and without buttons on the front. Under this was a closed, dark blue vest, fastened at the side rather than the front. The Zouave's trousers were of madder red wool, made without individual legs and ending just below the knees. A blue sash was wrapped about the waist, covering the top of the trousers, and a pair of gaiters secured the bottom of the trousers. The gaiters were covered at the top with leather greaves, or *jambières* (leather leggings worn over garters). For headgear, the Zouave wore a fez, wrapped originally in a green turban. Later the turban was made of white cloth. Ornamentation on these uniforms was limited to red tape edging on the jackets at the edges and cuffs, and on the body in the form of a false pocket known as a *tombeau*, shaped like a circle culminating in a stem topped with a trefoil. The *Tirailleurs Algériens* wore the same uniform, but in light blue with yellow trim.

In Crimea in 1854 and Italy in 1859, Zouave and Turco (the popular name for the native *Tirailleurs*) figured prominently in the campaigns. At the opening Crimean battle of the Alma, Zouaves bravely scaled the heights under Russian fire, and at the climactic battle of Sebastapol, it was again Zouaves who launched foolhardy assaults upon the Russian fortifications. In Italy, Zouaves and Turcos fought in the bloody battles of Magenta and Solferino, and they appeared in press releases, lithographs, and heroic oil renditions of the battles. Their bravery and exotic dress, along with stories of their notorious foraging and petty thievery, made them gallant rascals who captured the imagination of the European, and soon the American, public. Zouave soldiers figured

prominently in the illustrated American weeklies of the 1850s, which included sidebars and short features on Zouave antics and foibles. Perhaps the color and caprice of these soldiers were a seductive distraction in the normally staid life of the Victorian age. For whatever reason, the allure of the Zouave uniform reached the United States in the 1850s and took solid root.

It was not until 1860, however, that the Zouave movement reached its true zenith. That year, a highly trained Zouave drill team from Chicago, led by E. Elmer Ellsworth, undertook a national excursion, challenging local militia units to drill competitions, and appearing on the front pages of newspapers throughout the nation. Ellsworth's U.S. Zouave Cadets wore a uniform based upon, but not copied from, the French uniform: "A bright red chasseur cap with gold braid; light blue shirt with moire antique facings; dark blue jacket with orange and red trimmings; brass bell buttons, placed as close together as possible; a red sash and loose red trousers; russet leather leggings, buttoned over the trousers, reaching from ankle halfway to knee; and a white waistbelt."[1]

This flamboyant uniform actually had more circus than military in its ancestry, but Ellsworth's design influenced numerous imitators within the year, from the Albany Zouave Cadets to Baxter's and Gosline's Pennsylvania Zouaves, with their button-trimmed jackets. Elmer Ellsworth became a national hero. His Zouave Cadets disbanded after the tour, but many later became officers of volunteer Zouave regiments. In 1861, Ellsworth raised a regiment of Zouaves from New York City firemen and became the first national martyr,

Zouave uniform of Sgt. William D. Porter, Company K, 155th Pennsylvania Volunteers. This regiment was transformed into Zouaves in early 1864 by the acquiescence of the army Quartermaster Department, which economized by cannibalizing the remaining stock of imported French chasseur clothing. The trousers and leggings were enlarged, and jackets were cut from the hooded talmas. This uniform is a slate blue-gray in color, referred to in official documents as "French dark sky-blue kersey." Sergeant Porter wore this uniform when with the color guard at the battle of Five Forks, Virginia, in 1865. TROIANI COLLECTION.

killed by a prosecessionist after seizing a Confederate flag. His Zouave tour had sown the seeds that grew into dozens, if not hundreds, of militia and quasimilitary Zouave companies throughout the nation. Their uniforms were often poor imitations of the French originals or reflected an originality of design that probably would have embarrassed a French Zouave, but they became an integral part of the history of the uniforms of the war.

The first regiments of volunteer Civil War Zouaves wore a vast variety of uniforms. Hawkins' Zouaves of New York wore proper Zouave jackets and vests, but with dark blue trousers that, while baggy, were not of true Zouave proportions. Duryée's Zouaves, a highly professional set of volunteers, wore close copies of the true blue and red French uniform. Wallace's Zouaves of Indiana came to war in gray uniforms and kepis rather than "heathen" blue and red Zouave garb. Even Ellsworth's Fire Zouaves were originally uniformed in gray uniforms with red fire shirts. Wheat's Tiger Rifles of New Orleans had blue jackets and fezlike caps, but wore red shirts and white-and-blue-striped trousers. Baxter's Philadelphia Fire Zouaves came to war in short blue jackets ornamented on the edges with brass buttons, light blue trousers, and dark blue chasseur-style kepis. Coppen's Louisiana Zouaves, with many French-American volunteers, came close to the French, even to the use of *vivandières* (women licensed to act as sutlers in a regiment) to assist the soldiers.

The uniforms of these volunteers reflected the individuality of the regiments as much as they did the Zouave originals. They were procured in the initial rush to arms with public and private funding. In the North, the Federal government assumed the task of clothing the volunteers and attempted to standardize, but never eliminated, the Zouave uniform. In the South, the Zouave uniform disappeared in the scramble among state and central governments to procure and distribute clothing to the Confederate soldiers. In 1863, a second wave of Northern Zouaves was created in the Army of the Potomac, and new Zouave uniforms were fashioned for them. When the war ended in 1865, and the triumphant Armies of the Republic paraded in Washington, D.C., there were more regiments in Zouave uniform than there had been in the army of 1861. Zouaves fought in their distinctive uniforms in every major battle of the war. Their contributions are measured in the valiant dead they left upon those many fields.

In Europe, the chasseur could be a light infantryman or a light cavalryman. In the United States during the Civil War, only the light infantry chasseur's uniform was mimicked. The use of light infantry was indeed largely due to the colonial experience in North America. Irregular warfare in the vast forests of the New World reshaped the European style of warfare, as well as the uniforms worn by the Regulars of

A dark blue jacket with yellow-orange cording and small brass ball buttons worn by a member of the Boston Light Infantry, a well-known independent company in the Massachusetts Volunteer Militia. Written in the sleeve is the inscription "Worn at Fort Warren 1861." WEST POINT MUSEUM.

Europe. In Napoléon III's second empire, all infantry became light infantry, with quicker tactical movements, more open formations, and uniforms meant to reflect that style of warfare. In the 1850s, the *Chasseurs à Pied de la Garde Impériale,* or Foot Chasseurs of the Imperial Guard, wore a distinctive uniform that consisted of a short frock coat *(habit-tunique)* extending a few inches below the waist, vented at the bottom edge with a slit; "voluminous breeches" tucked into *jambières* and gaiters; and a low, plumed shako for headgear. For fatigue purposes, the chasseurs wore the distinctive kepi that had originated in the desert warfare of North Africa, known in the United States as the chasseur kepi.[2]

In 1860, as a part of the movement toward greater battlefield mobility, all French infantry were ordered into uniforms like those of the Imperial Guard Chasseurs. The short-skirted *habit-tunique* and baggy trousers were adopted, along with a new short leather shako. The *habit* was of dark

FIRST AT MANASSAS

The 11th New York, Ellsworth's Fire Zouaves, and J. E. B. Stuart's 1st Virginia Cavalry clashed in a brief but significant skirmish on Henry Hill at the battle of First Bull Run. The contrast in their uniforms and military careers is striking. The Fire Zouaves came to Manassas in dark blue Zouave jackets and trousers with red firemen's shirts, red and blue fezzes or havelock-covered red kepis, and, when worn, russet leather leggings. Many of these undisciplined firemen abandoned their Zouave jackets in the July heat, fighting in shirtsleeves. All, however, kept their M1855 rifles and rifle muskets, for they did come spoiling for a fight. They considered themselves a crack regiment, capable of slashing through the whole Confederate army.

Stuart's cavalrymen also considered themselves invincible, true heirs of the cavalier spirit, who would ride roughshod over a tyrant's mercenary hordes. They were uniformed in assorted clothing, from gray and black battle shirts to Stuart's own old, blue Federal uniform. Though armed with Sharps carbines and revolvers, the saber's cold steel still held great appeal to these novice warriors, and they charged the Zouaves with sabers flashing. The collision of the two regiments was brief, with few casualties, but the Zouaves were so shaken that they fled the field under a later crossfire.

Ellsworth's Fire Zouaves were never again an effective military unit. Within a year, they were a hopeless cause, and the regiment was disbanded. Stuart's warriors, on the other hand, became one of the Confederacy's best cavalry regiments. Their gray uniforms with black trim and broad-brimmed plumed hats became well known on many battlefields.

Although it is generally assumed that Zouave uniforms were flashy and elaborate, the hard-fighting men of David B. Birney's 23rd Pennsylvania Volunteer Infantry wore a rather simple uniform. With a short, open jacket sparsely trimmed with edgings of red yarn and loops at each cuff, as well as let into the shoulder seams, along with a dark blue vest, trousers, and cap, there was nothing flashy about the uniforms of this regiment. WEST POINT MUSEUM.

6TH NEW YORK VOLUNTEERS, WILSON'S ZOUAVES

What is a Zouave? Is it simply a soldier in a fancy uniform, or is it a soldier with an attitude? In the case of Billy Wilson's Zouaves—the 6th New York Volunteer Infantry—there were no fancy uniforms, but plenty of attitude. Organized by William Wilson, a New York City politician, from the "roughs and b'hoys" of the city, the 6th styled itself the Union Zouaves but was unable to provide Zouave uniforms for itself. Instead, upon signing the enlistment roll, each man was given "a new thick grey shirt, and a tricolor cockade for his breast." Wilson, a showman as well as politician, swore in his new regiment with a ceremony as rowdy as a political rally. Waving the American flag, Wilson called on his men to swear to support the flag and never flinch through blood or death. Waving their brown felt-brimmed hats or brandishing their seven-inch Bowie knives, Wilson's men responded with shouts of "Blood! Blood!" They had attitude.

What they did not have, in the beginning, though, was good leadership. Shipped to Florida in June 1861, the 6th New York did little except help man the guns of Fort Pickens. On October 9, 1861, a surprise Confederate attack upon the regiment's island camp caused a rout and the burning of their tents. It took Regular infantry to drive off the Rebel troops. Wilson's Zouaves needed a dose of discipline. After a purge of "its bad officers and soldiers," the regiment proved worthy of its initial attitude and served with credit in the XIX Corps against Port Hudson, Louisiana. Billy Wilson took his "b'hoys" home in June 1863.

TIMOTHY OSTERHELD

This kepi belonged to Pvt. Sullivan Wiley, Company I, 8th Massachusetts (Salem Zouaves—Salem Light Infantry). Wiley served with this unit from April 30 to August 1, 1861, when he joined the 12th Maine Volunteers. JOHN OCKERBLOOM COLLECTION.

SALEM ZOUAVES, 8TH MASSACHUSETTS VOLUNTEER MILITIA, 1861

By 1860, many of the old independent militia companies were feeling their age in that they suffered declining numbers and were losing popularity to more modern militia organizations. Among these well-established units was the venerable Salem Light Infantry, chartered by the state of Massachusetts in 1805. The Salem Light Infantry held a ban-

quet for Comdr. William Bainbridge of the U.S. frigate *Constitution* in 1813 in celebration of that ship's victories in the War of 1812. In the ensuing years, the company was prominent in all of the celebrations and parades, both in Salem and throughout the state. In 1859, as it tried to keep up with the fashions of the time, the company adopted the French

Zouave drill under the tutelage of its captain, Arthur F. Devereux. The next year, 1860, it hosted the U.S. Zouave Cadets of Elmer Ellsworth during their East Coast tour.

The initial uniform of the Salem Zouaves, as the company came to be known, was not a Zouave uniform. Instead, the men of the Salem Zouaves wore a closed shell jacket of medium blue, trimmed with imitation frogging in red on the breast, medium blue pants, and red fatigue caps. With the outbreak of the war, the company was placed in the 8th Regiment, Massachusetts Volunteer Militia, for three months' service as Company I (alternately recorded as Company J). The regiment left for Washington on April 18, 1861, and the Salem Zouaves under Captain Devereux found themselves providing part of the ship's crew sailing the USS *Constitution*

from Annapolis to the Brooklyn Navy Yard to save it from secessionists. The historic militia company had again done honor to a ship that has become a national treasure.

Returning south, the Salem Zouaves were stationed in Baltimore when they received their first true Zouave-style uniform, delivered on June 26, 1861. The jacket, vest, and pants were made of a navy blue woolen twill fabric with crimson trim. The cap had a red crown with dark blue band and was quartered with gold braid. An original uniform is in the collection of Salem's Essex Institute, and several photographs clearly preserve the unusual features of this Americanized Zouave garb. Armed with M1855 rifle muskets, the Salem Zouaves were examples of militia service in war, answering the first call for defense.

Officer's jacket and vest of the Salem Zouaves. The officers' clothing was trimmed with gold, in contrast to the red trim of the enlisted men. JOHN OCKERBLOOM COLLECTION.

11TH INDIANA ZOUAVES

Col. Lew Wallace, acting adjutant general of the state of Indiana, appointed himself the colonel of one of the six new three-month regiments assembling in Indianapolis in April 1861. Numbered the 6th through the 11th in memory of the five regiments raised for the war with Mexico, Wallace chose the final, the 11th, as his regiment. The men of this regiment wanted to be Zouaves from the start, and they were known as the 11th Regiment—Indiana Zouaves.

Wallace, a devout Christian who later wrote the novel *Ben Hur,* wanted "nothing of the flashy, Algerian colors" in his regiment. Instead, the 11th wore a conservative gray modified Zouave garb:

> Our outfit was of the tamest twilled goods, not unlike home made jeans—a visor cap, French pattern, its top of red cloth . . . ; a blue flannel shirt with open neck; a jacket Greekish in form, edged with narrow binding, the red scarcely noticeable; breeches baggy, but not petticoated; button gaiters connecting below the knees with the breeches, and strapped over the shoes. The effect was to magnify the men, though in line two thousand yards off they looked like a smoky ribbon long-drawn out.

Later the regiment received blue replacement Zouave uniforms of an entirely different style, which were worn through much of the war.

Wallace's Indiana Zouaves reorganized for three years' service in August 1861. They went on to serve in the Western Theater at such places as Shiloh and Vicksburg, and after transfer to the East, at Opequon and Cedar Creek. Wallace was promoted to major general, serving on the courts-martial of both the Lincoln conspirators and Andersonville commandant Henry Wirz.

PRIVATE COLLECTION

This flamboyant cap was worn by Gouverneur Kemble Warren as colonel of the 5th New York Volunteer Infantry, the famed Duryée Zouaves, between August 1861 and September 1862. In the painting A Picnic on the Hudson, *by Thomas Prichard Rossiter, he is seen lounging in a conspicuous pair of scarlet trousers and a cap such as this one.*

WEST POINT MUSEUM.

5TH NEW YORK VOLUNTEERS, DURYÉE ZOUAVES

Although constructed of surprisingly poor, shoddy wool, this corporal's jacket of the famed Duryée Zouaves— the 5th New York Volunteers—is heavily embellished with gold tape chevrons and trim. The 5th was one of the few volunteer regiments that maintained the Zouave dress throughout its entire term of service. TROIANI COLLECTION.

The 5th New York became one the Civil War's most famous regiments for many reasons, not the least of which was its prowess on the battlefield. Part of its success, however, came from the pride the men of the 5th felt over their distinctive dress. From the beginning, the regiment's officers concerned themselves with details of its uniforms as well as its training. At Fort Schuyler in New York, they voted upon the infantry manual for the regiment as well as making decisions about their uniform. The pants would be "red and large, no stripe, the Full Dress cap, the Col. Made a motion that it should be Scarlett & Blue trimmed with Gold according to Rank, of the Zouave style."

The enlisted Zouave uniform was first made by Devlin, Hudson & Co. of New York City, evidently in haste, for there was much dissatisfaction with its appearance and fit. The manufacturer blamed part of the problem on the fact that the Zouaves persisted in wearing regular trousers under the Zouave pants, destroying the fit. When William Howard "Bull Run" Russell, the English journalist, saw them in July,

he ridiculed their garb as "ill-made jackets" and "loose bags of red calico hanging from their loins." It was hardly a uniform to inspire great deeds, but Col. Abram Duryée pushed for better uniforms. By late summer, he had replaced the original uniforms with better-fitting and better-made close copies of the true French Zouave dress. He even succeeded in obtaining proper leather greaves, or *jambières,* to wear at the top of the white leggings over the bottom of the trousers. When the 5th New York was reviewed by Spanish general Juan Prim in June 1862, the Spaniard at first believed he had found a transplanted regiment of Frenchmen.

It was in these uniforms that the 5th New York made its gallant stands at Gaines' Mill and Second Bull Run, placing it forever in the "Fighting 500" regiments of the war. Uniforms may not make the soldier, but a regiment's *esprit de corps* can be inspired by many things, including its distinctive dress.

10TH NEW YORK VOLUNTEER INFANTRY, NATIONAL ZOUAVES

Providing uniforms for the Civil War soldier was always a demanding process for the quartermaster. Procuring and issuing sufficient clothing for the ever-increasing number of troops recruited for the war was taxing to a system based upon a peacetime establishment of a mere 16,000 men, but when the Federal volunteers demanded special regimental uniforms, quartermasters faced a procurement nightmare. The uniforms required for the 10th New York were a perfect example.

The 10th was recruited around a prewar organization known as the National Zouaves, which wore a "neat and attractive" Zouave uniform "affording perfect action of the limbs," and was expanded into a regiment under Col. Waters W. McChesney. The 10th's first wartime uniform was a hastily improvised "dark blue flannel costume, of the Zouave pattern, with grey fatigue caps." This uniform rapidly fell apart in active use, and sometime in June 1861, a new Zouave uniform of "the same pattern as the old, but of heavier cloth, the color being dark brown with red trimmings," was paid for by the state. In September, another new Zouave uniform was given to the regiment, this one beginning the practice of wearing light blue trousers with the Zouave jackets. These uniforms were evidently lost during the Peninsula campaign of spring 1862, when the regiment's baggage was burned during the evacuation of the army's base camp at White House Landing.

On September 5, 1862, an order was issued for the procurement of new Zouave uniforms manufactured by "Messer Wm. Seligman & Co. who made the old uniform," and once again the 10th was in a distinctive regimental uniform. With dark blue jackets, red vests, light blue trousers tucked into white leggings, and knapsacks painted with "10–NZ," the National Zouaves went back to war. From the bloody fields of Fredericksburg to the end of the war, there were veteran soldiers of the 10th New York in Zouave uniform. It would have been simpler to replace the 10th's uniforms with simple sack coats and forage caps, but the quartermasters of the Civil War understood the value of *esprit de corps* and of regiments such as the National Zouaves who possessed it.

WILLIAM RODEN

LOUISIANA ZOUAVE BATTALION, COPPEN'S ZOUAVES,1861

The mystique of the French Zouaves had taken a strong hold on the imagination of the young men who came forward to fight for the Union or the Confederacy in 1861. Given the long-standing French heritage of New Orleans, it was only natural that this city was the only one to send several companies of men dressed in true copies of Zouave attire to serve in the Confederate army. Whereas other localities in all corners of the South had Zouave companies among their troops, all the other uniforms only approximated that of the French Zouaves, and some companies boasted nothing but the title. Of the New Orleans companies, those of the 1st Louisiana Zouave Battalion, raised by Georges Augustus Gaston De Coppens, most closely resembled the true Zouave. The resemblance was more than simple appearance; the men of the battalion quickly gained a reputation as tough fighters.

As reported in the *New Orleans Commercial Bulletin:*

DAVID RANKIN, JR.

> The Richmond correspondent of the *Savannah Republican* thus speaks of our Zouaves: The roughest men I have seen on our side are the Louisiana Zouaves, about 600 strong, who have been at Pensacola. They are a tough, dare-devil, hardy looking set of fellows—excellent prototypes of the original French Zouaves. They have the regular Zouave uniform and that dashing rakish air supposed to belong to the originals. I don't wish "Old Abe" any worse fate than a consignment to their tender mercies. They are unquestionably the very spawn of war—that reckless breed that time of turmoil engender in malignant profusion. We have very few such soldiers in our army, however—less I presume than ever tainted any army the world has known. But it is one of the horrors of war to breed such characters.

The battalion served the Confederacy until the very last days of the war, seeing action from the Peninsula campaign of 1862 to the trenches of Petersburg in 1864–65. It is likely, however, that little of the color and distinction of the Zouave uniform was ever worn into battle. By November 4, 1861, the rigors of military life in the field had taken their toll. A requisition stating that "the Battalion is greatly in need of clothing not having received any since the 27th of March 1861, and is consequently entirely destitute" resulted in the battalion receiving a complete refitting, consisting of the following:

449 caps	898 flannel shirts	449 Jackets
449 overcoats	898 drawers	49 blankets
449 trousers	480 pr. Shoes	449 pants

Subsequent issues show no sign of the return to the grand uniforms in which they left for war. Within the battalion, however, the spirit of the Zouaves never died.

34TH OHIO VOLUNTEER INFANTRY, PIATT'S ZOUAVES

The Zouave volunteers raised in the West—Ohio, Indiana, Illinois, and Missouri—were not so gaudily dressed as their Eastern brethren. Wallace's Indiana Zouaves wore somber gray uniforms with scant red trim. Ohio's initial regiment of Zouaves was raised by Abram Sanders Piatt, a farmer and editor of the *Macacheek Press*. Piatt originally recruited the 13th Ohio Infantry, a ninety-day regiment that did not leave Ohio before its enlistment expired. The 34th Ohio, which later bore his name, never wore the baggy trousers or open oriental-style jacket of the true Zouave.

Called the 1st Ohio Zouaves, its sister regiment, the 54th, being the 2nd Zouaves, the 34th was organized at Camp Lucas, Ohio, but moved to Camp Dennison on September 1, 1861. Piatt was appointed its colonel on September 2. At Dennison, the regiment was hastily prepared for field service, there adopting its distinctive uniform and its nickname of Piatt's Zouaves. The 34th and 54th wore the same uniform, a short, dark blue jacket trimmed on the edges with red tape. Their sky blue trousers were trimmed with double stripes of red trim and tucked into russet leather leggings. The 34th wore its fezzes uncrushed, standing erect as in the Ottoman armies, the blue tassels dangling against their sides. Both regiments also wore a "three cornered hat with red tassel," similar to those worn by early Massachusetts troops.

The 34th spent its first winter in service on guard and scout duties against guerrillas in the Kanawha River Valley in what would soon become the state of West Virginia and remained there for much of the war. Originally armed with M1842 muskets, the regiment was armed with Enfield rifle muskets in 1863 and 1864. In 1864, it was moved to the Shenandoah Valley, fighting at Winchester, Opequon, and Fisher's Hill. The regiment's original colonel, Abram Piatt, was promoted to brigadier general of volunteers in April 1862. He fought in Virginia at Second Bull Run and later at Fredericksburg, where he was injured in a fall from horseback. Piatt then resigned his commission and returned to Ohio, where he resumed farming. Although never a fully rigged Zouave regiment, the 34th did serve as mounted infantry during its campaigns in the mountains of West Virginia, adding to the regiment's unusual history as Zouaves.

9TH NEW YORK VOLUNTEER INFANTRY, HAWKINS' ZOUAVES

Rush Hawkins was a meticulous man. It showed in the way he dressed and in the efforts he lavished later in life on his collection of rare books. It was only natural that when he created a regiment of volunteer Zouaves, he would be as attentive to the details of its organization.

This highly ordered regiment, the 9th New York Volunteers, originated from the New York Zouaves, a private military club formed in New York City on July 23, 1860. The New York Zouaves' by-laws, written by Hawkins, stated that "[t]here must, of necessity, be many absolute and positive rules, which must be carried out to the letter." Rush Hawkins was a man to enforce rules. When war broke out, Hawkins rushed to Albany to offer a regiment, which was sworn into state service on April 23 and mustered into Federal service as the 9th New York on May 4, 1861.

On his own initiative, Hawkins contracted for all the regimental equipment except the blankets, overcoats, and weapons. "When I commenced the formation of my Corps I had but one idea, and that was to make it a light Rifle regiment. Thus far the idea has been strictly addressed to in every minute particular. The accouterments are made after a pattern which I sent to France after, and are those which are now used by the three regiments of zouaves in the French Army. The material is a most excellent quality of flexible bridle leather." Hawkins paid attention to the details; as a result his regiment and its uniforms left an indelible mark upon the Federal armies.

After distinctive service with Burnside's expedition to South Carolina, the 9th joined the Army of the Potomac for the Maryland campaign. At the battle of Antietam, the 9th lost 240 of its 373 men in a charge that nearly broke the Confederate lines and reached Sharpsburg, giving the regiment's name a place in history. After Hawkins' Zouaves were mustered out of service on May 20, 1863, their uniform was

MRS. DONALD BLYN

chosen by the Federal quartermasters as a standard pattern for other Zouave regiments, such as the 17th and 164th New York. As Hawkins would say, "[A] uniform of glaring colors neither makes a man or a soldier." He should have known, for he created a regiment of soldiers.

18TH MASSACHUSETTS VOLUNTEER INFANTRY, 1861–62

Gen. Montgomery C. Meigs's Quartermaster Department was fully taxed trying to meet the demands of the growing Federal armies in the summer of 1861 and was eager to find a way to quickly supply the much-needed uniforms and equipment of these new troops. As an experiment, Meigs ordered 10,000 complete uniforms of the French chasseur, or light infantry, pattern from the firm of Alexis Godillot, the manufacturer for the French Army. It was hoped that these uniforms would solve some of the American supply problems and perhaps even set the patterns for redesigned Federal uniforms.

In what would today be considered a contracting miracle, the order was placed, and the uniforms and equipment were manufactured and actually shipped by late November 1861. These uniforms were remarkably complete and included every item a soldier needed, from "uniform coat with epaulets" to "blue cotton cravat" to "2 handkerchiefs." Moreover, the shipment included "hair tanned knapsacks" and a "*sac le petite,* containing five brushes for various purposes, needle case, with combs, thread, spool, cloak pin, and various other conveniences." It had to have been the most complete set of uniforms and equipment ever issued soldiers of the American army to that time.

The question of which regiments would receive them was settled with a drill competition, with three regiments of Gen. Fitz-John Porter's division of the Army of the Potomac winning the uniforms as prizes for the best performance. Among the winning regiments was the 18th Massachusetts. Unfortunately, the uniforms had been made in European sizes, too small to fit the American soldiers. Although larger sizes were evidently drawn from the remaining surplus, these elaborate uniforms were not at all popular with the soldiers, and as their novelty wore off, they were packed up and left in storage in Washington. Later in the war, bits and pieces of the uniforms were used for other purposes, but the 18th Massachusetts did not wear it to any of its battles with the Army of the Potomac.

Chasseur dress jacket (tunique, modèle 1860) worn by Jacob Martin of Company J, 62nd Pennsylvania Volunteer Infantry. With the exception of the cuff details and pewter eagle buttons, these extremely well-made garments were nearly identical to those produced for the French Army. JOHN HENRY KURTZ COLLECTION.

Snugly tailored fatigue jacket (habit-veste) of the imported French chasseur uniforms issued to the 18th Massachusetts and the 62nd and 83rd Pennsylvania Regiments. At least one regiment of New York's famed Excelsior Brigade received these uniforms in late 1862. TROIANI COLLECTION.

French Army pattern of 1858 cloth-covered tin canteen (bidon petit de 1 litre) imported with the 10,000 chasseur uniforms and equipment. The user was provided with two spouts, one for drinking and a narrow one for taking small sips on the march.
TROIANI COLLECTION.

The French infantry leather shakos of 1860 were the very latest pattern when purchased by the U.S. government. They were issued to the troops with full dress dark green-black feathers, while the field service green pom-poms remained in quartermaster stores. The 18th Massachusetts and 62nd and 83rd Pennsylvania do not seem to have been issued the brass eagle plates, but evidence shows at least one regiment of New York's famed Excelsior Brigade were. TROIANI COLLECTION.

65TH NEW YORK VOLUNTEER INFANTRY, 1861, 1ST U.S. CHASSEURS

Although not so exotic in appearance as the Zouaves of the French Army, chasseurs had their own distinctive garb, which also influenced the dress of American Civil War soldiers. Chasseur soldiers were light troops, originally tasked with the role of scouting and skirmishing against Regular troops, who moved and fought in solid formations. By the 1850s, the French Chasseurs of the Imperial Guard wore a new style uniform coat known as a *habit-veste*, which was simply a short frock coat, slit at the bottom edge on the side as vents. It provided more freedom of movement than the long-skirted frock coats worn by French infantry since the 1840s. For trousers, the Imperial Chasseurs wore baggy trousers tucked into *jambières* and leggings like those of the Zouaves.

Also like the Zouaves, chasseurs got considerable newspaper coverage. Woodcut illustrations of the *Chasseurs de Vincennes* drill were nearly as common as charging Zouaves. It was understandable that these French uniforms were copied along with the Zouave dress. The 65th New York adopted a uniform based upon the French style: "Their uniform is neat, military and allowing free motion to the soldiers. It is army blue, chasseur jacket, trimmed with light blue braid, cadet gray pantaloons and gray caps." The light blue braid ran along the edges of the coat, with trefoil knots on each cuff and sprouting from the corners of the vents created by slitting the sides of the coat skirts. Along with the gray kepis issued in New York, the regiment received M1858 uniform hats, more popularly called Hardee hats, trimmed with bugle horn insignia with the numeral 1 in the loop, and sky blue hat cords to match the coat trim.

The 65th New York went to war in September 1861, spending most of its term in the VI Corps of the Army of the Potomac. Present at all major battles from the Peninsula

PRIVATE COLLECTION

through the Appomattox campaign, it lost a total of 146 men in combat or captivity. One of its colonels, Alexander Shaler, received the Medal of Honor for bravery at Marye's Heights. At war's end, all four of the men who had led the 65th as colonel had been promoted to general.

76TH PENNSYLVANIA VOLUNTEER INFANTRY, KEYSTONE ZOUAVES

RICK AND JOAN DAVIES

The Zouaves of the 76th Pennsylvania, formed as the Keystone Zouaves, wore a unique variation of traditional dress. The 76th's original Zouave dress, which was not well documented, was replaced with regulation Federal clothing. It was not until November 1862 that its colonel, DeWitt C. Strawbridge, requested a new set of Zouave uniforms. These were supplied by Philadelphia's Schuylkill Arsenal and included light blue trousers, dark blue fezzes, and gray false vest fronts sewn to the jacket fronts. The regiment seems to have retained this uniform for dress throughout most of its remaining service, with photographs showing the use of veterans' stripes late in the war.

The 76th was on the Carolina coast for much of its military service, first garrisoning Hilton Head, South Carolina. Its first major combat came on July 11, 1863, in the form of assaults on Fort Wagner, where it fought its way to the parapets. The regiment lost 180 men, but made a second assault a week later. In that attack, Brig. Gen. George C. Strong was fatally wounded alongside the flag of the 76th. The regiment went on to Virginia, where it fought through Grant's Virginia campaign of 1864 at Cold Harbor, the Crater, and Petersburg. Transferred to the South again, the 76th was in the operations against Fort Fisher in 1865. By war's end, the regiment had lost 9 officers and 161 men killed or mortally wounded.

53RD NEW YORK VOLUNTEERS, D'EPINEUIL ZOUAVES

The 53rd New York Infantry was organized in New York City in the fall of 1861 by Col. Lionel J. D'Epineuil, a former officer in the French Army. The recruiting went forward at a slow pace, despite the fact that the colonel had received permission to outfit his men in the uniform of the French Zouaves of the Imperial Guard. The regiment eventually attracted men from other parts of the state, mostly of French descent, but also included one company of American Indians from the Tuscarora Reservation.

The New York City newspapers seemed to take particular interest in the uniform of the 53rd. "The uniform is that of the Blue Zouaves of France, which consists of dark blue jacket, trimmed with yellow braid, vest of the same, and full pants of light blue, red fez, with blue tassel and duck leggings. The cloth will be of the best quality, as good, in fact, as is used in the French army, and not the cheap flannel that was hitherto given some of our Zouaves."

"The uniform of the men is an exact copy of the 6th Regiment Imperial Zouaves of France, and is to be completed by Messers Brooks Bros., by special contract with the War Department. It consists of red fez cap with long yellow tassel, dark blue jacket trimmed with bright yellow braid, blue sash, and yellow and black leggings and duck gaiters." All of this amounted to a regiment that closely resembled the original French.

The regiment left New York on November 18, 1861. The men had been armed with the Enfield rifle musket and standard accoutrements. From all appearances, the 53rd New York would make a good account of itself once it reached the seat of war. But problems appeared almost from the start. It was apparent that the officers of the regiment had been in the habit of ignoring the condition of the men under their command. Desertions became a continual problem.

RONALD AND JULIE MARRA

Government-issue contract Zouave fez made for the 62nd New York Volunteers, the Anderson Zouaves. These caps were unlined and distinctively trimmed with a yellowish gold tape along the bottom edge. TROIANI COLLECTION.

These white linen leggings were worn by a soldier in the 76th Pennsylvania Volunteer Infantry (Keystone Zouaves). They are typical of those issued by the Quartermaster Department during the mid- to late-war period. TROIANI COLLECTION.

A pair of leather greaves (jambières) worn by a soldier of the 76th Pennsylvania Volunteer Infantry (Keystone Zouaves). Greaves were worn over the tops of the leggings and served to keep the trousers secured. TROIANI COLLECTION.

After being placed on board a ship for what was to be trip of several days to Hatteras, the men finally disembarked thirty-four days later at Annapolis after a series of botched attempts at landing. After this length of time, the condition of the entire command had deteriorated to a point that was beyond repair. Within a few days, nearly 400 men were no longer present for duty. An inspection of the regiment found "rifle muskets in bad order . . . uniforms very dirty, and in many cases, filthy." The fine uniforms were found to be so infested with lice that many had to be burned.

It may be that competent leadership could have salvaged the situation, but the 53rd New York was disbanded on March 21, 1862. Some of the men enlisted in the Regular army, while others were transferred to volunteer regiments from their home state.

RED DEVILS

Months of campaigning had taken the shine off the bright uniforms of the 5th New York Volunteer Infantry. It had not dulled the fighting edge of the men wearing them, however, as the gallant stand of the Duryée Zouaves at Gaines' Mill on June 27, 1862, proved. With Color Sgt. Francis Spelman felled with heat stroke, Sgt. John H. Berrian planted the regimental flag and dared the Confederates to take it. The Zouaves kept their flags but were so decimated by intense fire that they were pulled out of the line. Before they left the field, however, their colonel ordered them to count off and realign ranks to fill in for 162 fallen comrades.

The brilliant red of their trousers was offset by the dark blue of their Zouave jackets and vests. In many ways, the 5th's uniform was one of the closest American copies of the French original. An American touch, however, was found in the gilt lace chevrons and gold-edged trim of the regiment's noncommissioned officers. Red sashes edged with light blue, white leggings topped with yellow leather *jambières,* and red fezzes wrapped with white turbans—all the exotic trappings of the true Zouave soldier—marked the 5th New York as a distinctive regiment, but their performance at Gaines' Mill marked them as soldiers.

114TH PENNSYLVANIA VOLUNTEER INFANTRY, COLLIS ZOUAVES

On July 3, 1863, as he rode across the battlefield of the previous day at Gettysburg, an English officer "present with the Confederate Army" noted among the dead "a number of Yankees dressed in bad imitations of the Zouave costume." The dead this disdainful Englishman was referring to were from the 114th Pennsylvania, the Collis Zouaves.

The 114th was originally raised as the *Zouaves d'Afrique* by Charles H. T. Collis, a Philadelphia lawyer, to serve as a bodyguard to Maj. Gen. N. P. Banks. This company was mus-

tered in and sent to Fort Delaware in August 1861, where it was thoroughly drilled in Zouave tactics. The *Zouaves d'Afrique* fought in several battles and skirmishes as an independent company with such success that in the summer of 1862, Collis began to recruit additional companies for an entire regiment of Zouaves.

At the end of August 1862, Collis's new regiment was in Washington, and the 114th Pennsylvania began its life as a regiment in the Army of the Potomac. It was a fully rigged

From the start, Collis's Zouaves wore a well-designed uniform patterned after that of French Zouaves. The original company was joined by nine new companies and expanded into the 114th Pennsylvania Volunteer Infantry. Although officers wore standard frock coats, they did have the red trousers and caps of Zouaves. WEST POINT MUSEUM.

Uniform of the 114th Pennsylvania Volunteers worn by Thadeus Paxton of Company F. This famed regiment, also known as the Collis Zouaves, wore a jacket with light blue cuffs and chasseur trousers made of brick red imported French Army cloth. Paxton died of disease in January 1863. TROIANI COLLECTION.

Zouave regiment, with uniforms made of cloth imported from France, but with an American twist. Its trousers, of proper madder red cloth, were not the full French Zouave style, but made less baggy and as actual trousers so they could be worn without leggings if needed. The short, open blue jacket was trimmed in red like the French originals but had light blue cuffs as well. Fezzes and turbans, for full dress, completed the Collis Zouaves' unique uniform.

The regiment participated in every major battle of the

Army of the Potomac, and at Fredericksburg in December 1862, Collis himself received the Medal of Honor for his actions in leading his Zouaves in deadly battle. It was Gettysburg, however, that decimated the regiment. Although only thirteen were dead or mortally wounded there, eighty-six were wounded and sixty captured or missing. Much reduced by their casualties, the 114th was made provost guard of the Army of the Potomac Headquarters, serving with distinction through the remainder of the war.

95TH PENNSYLVANIA VOLUNTEERS, GOSLINE ZOUAVES

The 95th Pennsylvania Infantry, the Gosline Zouaves, was one of several regiments raised in and around Philadelphia in the fall of 1861 to receive what the U.S. Army termed a special uniform. The 95th was able to retain much of this distinctive dress for its entire term of service, being resupplied as necessary by the Quartermaster Department. In addition, in the final months of the war, this regiment was one of the very few selected to receive and try the new style accoutrements designed and patented by Col. William D. Mann, formerly of the 7th Michigan Cavalry. These accoutrements were designed to ease the burden on the individual soldier by redistributing the weight of the cartridge box. The concept had some merit and was an improvement over conventional equipment. The ending of the war, however, with the resulting vast surplus of old-style equipment, ended any chance that Colonel Mann's idea would be adopted by the army.

The uniform of the 95th remained largely unchanged from that received in 1861. The initial outfit had been contracted for by the Quartermaster Department from the Philadelphia clothing house of Rockhill and Wilson. The original uniform was described by a member of Company A as follows:

> The regimental uniform was of the zouave pattern, and differed but little from other zouave organizations—Birney's and Baxter's—then forming in the city. . . . [It] consisted of the best material, heavy marine cloth. The jacket . . . was rounded at the waist, and trimmed with broad and narrow scarlet braid. Down each side was a row of brass buttons, adding greatly to its beauty and finish. The pants were of full length, not so wide as the regular Zouave Petticoat but just wide enough to harmonize with the pleated waist, in broad folds. The over shirt was of Navy flannel, with silver plated buttons corresponding with those on the jacket, but several sizes smaller. The cap was the McClellan style, braided with narrow scarlet braid. A pair of leather leggings nearly reaching the knees finished the uniform.

Photographs show that by late 1864, the pleated trousers and the cap were replaced by standard-issue uniform items, but the jacket and the vest remained. The 95th Pennsylvania served its entire term of service with the Army of the Potomac. From September 1862 until muster out, they were part of the famous VI Corps.

PRIVATE COLLECTION

As an interesting side note, a paper from after the war gives a glimpse of how contract operations worked prior to worries about conflict of interest. On August 21, 1861, Company A's recruiting station was opened over the clothing establishment of Rockhill and Wilson.

72ND PENNSYLVANIA VOLUNTEER INFANTRY, BAXTER'S FIRE ZOUAVES

Nearly every fire company in Philadelphia provided recruits for Col. DeWitt Clinton Baxter's new regiment raised in the summer of 1861. As a result, the regiment became known as Baxter's Fire Zouaves.

Their uniform was a modified and slightly less ornate version of that worn by Ellsworth's militia Zouaves, with sixteen ball buttons along each edge of the jacket, and light blue trousers that were not the full trousers of a true Zouave. Still, it was part of their identity as a regiment, and in June 1863, a month before finding themselves in the center of the fight to repulse Pickett's Charge at Gettysburg, they received new Zouave uniforms.

The 72nd had been seriously bloodied first at Antietam, where they had suffered 58 deaths in the fight for the West Woods. At Gettysburg, with only 473 men in the line, the regiment lost 64 dead or mortally wounded and an additional 125 wounded. The remnants of the gallant charge retreated to Seminary Ridge that day, leaving the exhausted survivors of Baxter's Fire Zouaves to help hold the Union line in what has been called the turning point of the Civil War. They fought on through the Wilderness and the siege of Petersburg before mustering out in 1864. After the war, many of these veteran soldier-firemen revived Baxter's Fire Zouaves as a militia unit, continuing the Fire Zouave tradition in peace as well as war.

Pvt. Edward S. Fulton of the 72nd Pennsylvania Volunteers, the Baxter Zouaves, was wearing this red-trimmed jacket when shot three times during the battle of Antietam. He was taken to a field hospital where, considered to be a hopeless case, he suffered unattended for three days. After a long recovery at Smoketown Hospital, he mustered out. He lived at home until 1879, when a medical procedure on one of his war wounds proved fatal. TROIANI COLLECTION.

Government-issue Zouave fez worn by Sgt. James D. Pitcher of the 146th New York Volunteers. Pitcher wore it with the brim turned up for a snugger fit, a common practice. TROIANI COLLECTION.

Bright red chasseur trousers worn by Sgt. Alexander Barnie, Jr., of the famed Brooklyn 14th. Well known for their picturesque garb, soldiers of the regiment searching for bodies of their friends killed at First Manassas nine months earlier wrote, "Yet here we find, unburied, the bodies of our comrades, clearly distinguishable by the peculiar uniform of the regiment. The unmistakable red pants and loose blue jacket are easily recognized." (BROOKLYN DAILY EAGLE, MARCH 21, 1862.) COLLECTION OF NEW YORK STATE DIVISION OF MILITARY AND NAVAL AFFAIRS.

146TH NEW YORK VOLUNTEER INFANTRY

After the fierce fighting of July 2, 1863, one officer remarked that the rocky slopes of Little Round Top "seemed to be covered with corpses in light blue Zouave uniforms." These were the dead of Garrard's Tigers, the 146th New York, raised in Oneida County, New York, in 1862. Col. Kenner Garrard's regiment was placed in the V Corps; and when it was determined to honor the memory of the departed 5th New York, Duryée's Zouaves, by creating new regiments of Zouaves from line infantry, the 146th became the first to receive new uniforms in June 1863—just in time for the battle of Gettysburg.

Technically, the 146th did not get Zouave uniforms, but the yellow-trimmed light blue uniforms of the *Tirailleurs Algériens,* or Turcos, of the French Colonial Army. Made exactly like the uniforms of the European Zouaves except for color, the new uniforms of the 146th were indeed unique in all the Federal armies. Attractive and serviceable, the uniforms were not without problems. Soon it was noticed that the yellow lace trim faded quickly, and the Zouave leggings were made improperly so that they lapped to the front and snagged easily when passing through brush. Still, it was a distinctive uniform, marking an exceptional regiment.

After their successful defense of Little Round Top in July 1863, the 146th and the other regiments of the Zouave Brigade of the V Corps found themselves embroiled in the Virginia Wilderness in May 1864. There the Tigers lost 312 men, 65 of whom, including the regiment's colonel and lieutenant colonel, were killed or mortally wounded.

165TH NEW YORK VOLUNTEER INFANTRY, 1863

The severe losses within the 5th New York in its battles in 1862 made it necessary to recruit new members, and the 5th's reputation made that recruiting easy. So easy, in fact, that more recruits were signed up than were needed, and a second battalion was formed, becoming the 165th New York. The 2nd Battalion Duryée Zouaves were shipped to the West, serving with the XIX Army Corps in the Department of the Gulf from January 1863 to July 1864. At the siege of Port Hudson on the Mississippi, the 165th joined in a doomed assault that resulted in the loss of a third of the battalion, including two color-bearers, and the mortal wounding of its commander, Lt. Col. Abel Smith, Jr. In July 1864, the battalion was transferred to Washington to serve in the Shenandoah Valley and later Georgia and the Carolinas. Never as famous as the 5th, the 2nd Battalion still had an impressive record in its nearly three years of service.

The Zouaves of the 2nd Battalion wore basically the same uniform as the original Duryée Zouaves. The distinctive blue and red uniforms of the two regiments of Duryée Zouaves differed only in that the 2nd Battalion wore blue-tasseled fezzes rather than the yellow of the 5th, and the 165th often wore plain sashes rather than the blue-bound red sashes of the original regiment. It was a uniform that spanned four years and all major theaters of the war.

PRIVATE, COMPANY G, 109TH PENNSYLVANIA INFANTRY, APRIL 1863

The 109th Pennsylvania, originally known as the Curtin Light Guard, was one of two regiments raised in Philadelphia that received a special uniform with a coat similar to that of the French chasseur. The other regiment, the 90th Pennsylvania, also had the distinction of being the only regiment that received uniforms supplied by the United States with a button design unique to that regiment. Other than the buttons, those of the 109th being standard army issue, the uniforms of the two regiments differed only in the trim. Whereas the 90th received coats and trousers with a cord or welt of regulation infantry blue, those of the 109th were trimmed with a cord made of individual strands of red, white, and blue yarn twisted together in a candy stripe pattern. Like the buttons of the 90th, this trim was worn only by this one regiment.

The 109th began recruiting in December 1861, two months after the 90th, and remained in the city drilling and filling its ranks until leaving for Washington in May 1862. It is interesting to note that of the regiments Pennsylvania sent to the field, the vast majority of those dressed in what the army termed "special uniforms" came from Philadelphia or its immediate area. The location in that politically important city of the U.S. Army's main clothing facility, Schuylkill Arsenal, as well as several of the country's major ready-to-wear clothing manufacturers, certainly had something to do with this. In most cases, these uniforms were supplied to those regiments throughout their term of service. The 109th was no exception. Initially many of the nonregulation uniforms were contracted from and supplied by one of several Philadelphia clothing houses. Those of the 90th and the 109th were, however, manufactured by the government, with the exception of an initial issue of "Zouave caps," which photographic evidence indicates were not resupplied. From the beginning, the 109th was armed with the M1861 rifle musket. The close proximity of the Alfred Jenks & Son factory, which by November 1861 was manufacturing the

Bridesburg contract model '61, makes it likely that the regiment was armed with these.

An interesting sidelight to the history of the 109th Pennsylvania appears in an order written to the headquarters of Franz Sigel's division in June 1862, detailing items to be carried in the field. It reads in part, "The knapsack is necessary . . . but this could be dispensed with in favor of the 'shelter tent' now in use in the 109th Pa. Vols. 1st Brigade, which with the Talma [cape] and proper straps could answer the purpose of a knapsack."

155TH PENNSYLVANIA VOLUNTEER INFANTRY

The 155th Pennsylvania Infantry did not begin its military life as a Zouave regiment. Recruited in western Pennsylvania and organized at Camp Howe near Pittsburgh during September 1862, the 155th was trained and equipped as a standard infantry regiment. First armed with Belgian rifles and later with M1842 muskets, at Gettysburg the men of the regiment scoured the battlefield to supply themselves with M1861 rifle muskets.

In the late summer and fall of 1863, as part of Kenner Garrard's 3rd Brigade, 2nd Division of the V Corps, the 155th was presented with Zouave uniforms as a tribute to the regiment's excellence in drill. The new uniform was evidently a source of pride: "The exchange to the zouave uniform from the plain infantry uniform was enjoyed immensely by the men . . . not only on account of their having earned the recognition, but also because of the great beauty of the uniform and the greater comfort and other advantages it possessed." This new uniform had an interesting history, for it was not a standard French style. The parsimonious Quartermaster Department had decided to use up the surplus French chasseur uniforms purchased earlier in the war by giving the 155th the blue-gray chasseur trousers from those sets and fabricating jackets from the same-color talmas, or capes, from the same lot. With bright yellow *tombeaux*, or false pockets, and trim and false vest fronts sewn to the jackets, the 155th had a unique Zouave uniform fabricated with an American twist.

NATIONAL CIVIL WAR MUSEUM, HARRISBURG, PENNSYLVANIA

The 90th Pennsylvania Volunteers (National Guards) was the only regiment in the Union army to have its own distinctive button, and the Quartermaster Department in Philadelphia contracted with the firm of William G. Mintzler to supply them throughout the war.

(NATIONAL ARCHIVES, RECORD GROUP 92, ENTRY 2195, BOOK 3.) EARL J. COATES COLLECTION.

The 155th served with the 140th and 146th New York, which also had unique uniforms, as part of Gen. Romeyn B. Ayres's Zouave Brigade in 1864. All three regiments suffered heavy casualties in the battle of the Wilderness, but the 155th suffered greater losses in the assault on Petersburg in June. For the remainder of the war, the men of the 155th fought proudly in their Zouave uniforms, and the last Federal soldier killed before Lee's surrender at Appomattox was a Zouave of the 155th Pennsylvania.

33RD NEW JERSEY VOLUNTEER INFANTRY, 2ND ZOUAVES

Not all Zouave regiments were raised in the first year of the war. Several were created later, such as the 33rd and 35th New Jersey Regiments—both recruited in the late summer of 1863—which were uniformed as Zouaves. Their uniforms were a recruiting ploy, and although the U.S. Quartermaster Department did not favor nonstandard uniforms,

they relented when fancy uniforms could help induce recruits to the colors. The Zouave uniform of the 33rd was based on that of the old Hawkins' Zouaves of New York, featuring the dark blue, short open jacket, Zouave vest, and narrow dark blue trousers gathered into black leather leggings. The deep red trim adorning these garments could not be called flashy, and the uniform was indeed distinctive without being outlandish. A dark blue chasseur cap like that of the 95th Pennsylvania, a Zouave regiment raised in 1861, replaced the Hawkins' Zouaves' red fez, again making for a less exotic uniform.

The 33rd was shipped to the Western Army of the Cumberland in the fall of 1863 to serve with the XX Corps under Gen. William Tecumseh Sherman. Garbed as Zouaves, its officers in frock coats with red silk braid worked into trefoils on the cuffs and its men in their subdued uniforms, the 33rd spent its first months in service guarding bridges and doing fatigue duties, which took a toll on their uniforms. Replacements were requested by the regiment's colonel, George W. Mindil, in January 1864, before the spring campaign. Because they were distinctive, the replacement uniforms could not be readily supplied, and the regiment was "compelled to take the field in mixed dress, and as the campaign progressed the wants of the men were supplied from time to time with the regulation uniform." By late summer, the 33rd no longer wore its Zouave uniform, and Mindil informed the Quartermaster Department that any surplus Zouave clothing in store could be "passed over to some other regiment wearing this especial dress, say the 35th New Jersey or 17th New York . . . of this Army."

The quartermaster general was delighted, and Montgomery Meigs replied that if "all troops would adopt the regular uniforms no such delay [in supply] would ensue, and, it is believed that they would be as comfortably clothed." No longer Zouaves, but now battle-hardened veterans, the 33rd marched with Sherman's armies from Georgia to the Grand Review in Washington, mustering out on July 17, 1865.

Zouave sash belonging to Cpl. James Young of the 44th New York Volunteers, People's Ellsworth Regiment. Young was killed in action on May 27, 1862, at Hanover Courthouse, Virginia. COLLECTION OF NEW YORK STATE DIVISION OF MILITARY AND NAVAL AFFAIRS.

5th New York Veteran Infantry, 1864

In May 1863, the original 5th New York Regiment of Infantry, Duryée's Zouaves, was mustered out upon the expiration of its term of service. The regiment had fought with the Army of the Potomac for two years and gained such stature that a brigade of Zouaves was added to the V Corps in honor of its service. It was natural, then, that there was an attempt to revive Duryée's Zouaves as a veteran regiment. Enough veterans of the original regiment were reenlisted for four companies, and additional recruits were found from other regiments. Still, it was not until May 1864 that the regiment, later brought to full strength through the addition of a battalion of men from the 12th and 84th New York, joined the Army of the Potomac in its Virginia campaigns.

Like the original 5th New York, the veteran 5th was fully uniformed as Zouaves. Their initial dress consisted of a medium rather than dark blue Zouave jacket, gray shirt, leather leggings, and red fez with white turban. Its red trousers, cut more in the chasseur style than the Zouave, were trimmed with yellow cord around the pockets in imitation of the French. In typical Zouave fashion, the cartridge box was worn on the waist belt rather than from a shoulder belt. Their second uniform featured a dark blue Zouave jacket of the Hawkins' Zouave pattern, with a dark blue vest, baggier trousers, and white leggings with leather *jambières.* One soldier, who had originally called the Zouave uniform a "horror of horrors," so changed his tune that in May 1865 he wrote, "The Fifth drew a new uniform to-day,—Zouave, of course,—and they look very fine; it will be the crack regiment in the Review to-morrow."

For its whole period of service, the 5th New York Veterans fought in the V Corps of the Army of the Potomac. The regiment fought at Bethesda Church (Cold Harbor), the siege of Petersburg, Five Forks, and Appomattox. In all, it suffered 405 battle casualties. Its career was by no means so glorious as that of the original Duryée Zouaves, but it saw the war to its conclusion.

PAUL J. SCHEIRL

National Archives, Record Group 94, Regiment Papers, 53rd New York Infantry.

74TH NEW YORK VOLUNTEER INFANTRY, 1861

New York Tribune, August 13, 1861, 8.

Frederick P. Todd, *American Military Equipage, 1851–1872*, vol. 2 (n.p.: Chatham Square, 1983).

William F. Fox, *Regimental Losses in the American Civil War, 1861–1865* (Albany, N.Y.: Albany Publishing Co., 1889).

Mark Mayo Boatner III, *The Civil War Dictionary* (New York: David McKay, 1959).

62ND NEW YORK VOLUNTEER INFANTRY, ANDERSON ZOUAVES

Bureau of Military Statistics, *Fifth Annual Report* (New York: Weed, Parsons, 1868), 115–16.

Frederick Phisterer, *New York in the War of the Rebellion 1861 to 1865* (Albany, N.Y.: J. B. Lyon, 1912).

Roger Sturcke, "62nd Regiment, New York Volunteer Infantry (Anderson's Zouaves), 1861–1865," *Military Collector and Historian* 35, no. 1 (spring 1983): 32–33.

Collections of the Smithsonian Institution.

114TH PENNSYLVANIA VOLUNTEER INFANTRY, COLLIS ZOUAVES

Frank H. Taylor, *Philadelphia in the Civil War* (Philadelphia, 1913).

Philadelphia Evening Bulletin, November 3, 1864.

Frank Rauscher, *Music on the March* (Philadelphia: Wm. F. Fell, 1892).

Michael J. McAfee, "114th Pennsylvania: The Collis Zouaves," *Military Images* 13, no. 1 (July–August 1991): 29.

95TH PENNSYLVANIA VOLUNTEERS, GOSLINE ZOUAVES

National Archives, Record Group 94, Regimental Papers, 95th Pennsylvania Infantry.

G. Norton Galloway, *The Ninety-fifth Pennsylvania Volunteers ("Gosline's Pennsylvania Zouaves") in the Sixth Corps* (Philadelphia, 1884).

U.S. Army, Military History Institute, Carlisle, Pa., Photographic Collection of Soldiers of the 95th Pennsylvania Volunteers.

72ND PENNSYLVANIA VOLUNTEER INFANTRY, BAXTER'S FIRE ZOUAVES

Charles H. Banes, *A History of the Philadelphia Brigade* (Philadelphia: J. B. Lippincott, 1876).

Michael J. McAfee, "72nd Regiment, Pennsylvania Volunteer Infantry (Baxter's Fire Zouaves)," *Military Images* 11, no. 6 (May–June 1990): 27.

146TH NEW YORK VOLUNTEER INFANTRY

Thomas W. Hyde, *Following the Greek Cross* (Boston: Houghton Mifflin, 1894), 149.

Mary Genevie Brainard, *Campaigns of the 146th Regiment* (New York: G. P. Putnam's Sons, 1915).

Michael J. McAfee, "The 146th New York Volunteer Infantry," *Military Images* 18, no. 1 (July–August 1996): 35

165TH NEW YORK VOLUNTEER INFANTRY, 1863

John A. Vanderbilt, John A. Murray, and Peter Biegel, *History of the Second Battalion Duryée Zouaves, One-Hundred Sixty-Fifth Regiment, New York Volunteer Infantry* (New York, 1905).

Thomas S. Townsend, *Honors of the Empire State in the War of the Rebellion* (New York: A. Lovell, 1889).

PRIVATE, COMPANY G, 109TH PENNSYLVANIA INFANTRY, APRIL 1863

National Archives, Record Group 92, Quartermaster Consolidated Correspondence File, Pennsylvania.

Ibid., entry 2182, Miscellaneous Records Schuylkill Arsenal, Letter Sent by Military Store Keeper, July 10, 1862.

Ibid., Record Group 156, M-12281, Quarterly Returns of Ordnance and Ordnance Stores on Hand in Regular and Volunteer Organizations.

Ibid., Record Group 94, Regimental Order and Letter Book, 109th Pennsylvania Infantry, June 8, 1862.

155TH PENNSYLVANIA VOLUNTEER INFANTRY

155th Regimental Association, *Under the Maltese Cross* (Pittsburgh, 1910).

Don Troiani and Brian Pohanka, *Don Troiani's Civil War* (Mechanicsburg, Pa.: Stackpole Books, 1995).

William F. Fox, *Regimental Losses in the American Civil War, 1861–1865.* (Albany, N.Y.: Albany Publishing Co., 1889).

33RD NEW JERSEY VOLUNTEER INFANTRY, 2ND ZOUAVES

National Archives, Record Group 94, Regimental Letter Book, 33rd New Jersey Volunteers.

Ibid., Record Group 92, Quartermaster Records, vol. 23.

Frederic Ray, Jr., Roger G. Sturcke, and Michael J. McAfee, "33rd Regiment, New Jersey Volunteer Infantry, '2nd Zouaves,' 1863–1865," *Military Collector and Historian* 31, no. 3 (fall 1979): 128–29.

5TH NEW YORK VETERAN INFANTRY, 1864

Robert Tilney, *My Life in the Army* (Philadelphia: Ferris and Leach, 1912).

Don Troiani et al., *Don Troiani's Soldiers in America, 1754–1865* (Mechanicsburg, Pa.: Stackpole Books, 1998).

17TH NEW YORK VETERAN VOLUNTEERS

National Archives, Record Group 92, entry 320, vol. 22, Quartermaster Records.

William B. Westervelt, *Lights and Shadows of Army Life* (Marlboro, N.Y.: C. H. Cochrane, 1886).

Special Branches and General Officers

THE HISTORIES OF THE GREAT ARMIES OF THE CIVIL War that maneuvered and fought for four bloody years rarely mention the multitude of support personnel without whose efforts no victory would have been possible. In the U.S. Army in 1861, these included the Adjutant General's, Judge Advocate's, Inspector General's, Quartermaster, Subsistence, Pay, and Ordnance departments; Engineers and Topographical Engineers corps; and the chief signal officer. The Confederate army, as established in 1861, included the Adjutant and Inspector General's, Quartermaster, Commissary General's, and Medical departments. Also established were two bureaus, Ordnance and Signal, as well as a Corps of Engineers. To a great extent, the officers and men of the staff departments and corps were some of the most dedicated and professional soldiers to serve either the Union or the Confederacy. So, too, were the men who marched with the army as pioneers; filled a vital role as signalmen; or, in the case of the Federal army, served in the Veteran Reserve Corps. It is true that in every service there were those who failed to fulfill their duties due to incompetence, intemperance, or dishonesty. It is a sad fact that these few men were often the ones who received the most attention in postwar writing. Confederate general Thomas Neville Waul, in an undated wartime report on the organization and administration of the special branches within the Confederate Army, summarized the service of the vast majority of these soldiers in a tribute that could apply as well to their counterparts in the Federal army. "The labors of these Departments penetrate the entire military establishment, breathe life into the army, nurture its growth, give it strength and efficiency in the field, maintaining its health, and facilitating its movements; vigilant, prepared and present, it moves unnoticed amid the stirring events of the field, and obscured by the dust and smoke of combat it remains unobserved even while collecting the fruits of victory."[1]

The uniforms of the special branches, both officers and enlisted men, were the same as those worn by the combat soldiers they supported. As a general rule, only the color of the trim and/or insignia set them apart. The exception was the Federal Veteran Reserve Corps, whose enlisted men wore a jacket made of the same sky blue material as the standard-issue trousers. Some members of the Veteran Reserves also received black cavalry greatcoats.[2] Rarely seen is the prescribed uniform for officers of the Veteran Reserves. Regulations called for them to wear a sky blue frock coat, with dark blue velvet collar and cuffs, and sky blue trousers with two

Embroidered officer's hat badge of the Signal Corps, worn by Pvt. Henry R. Congdon. With no regulation enlisted man's device authorized, Private Congdon obtained an officer's badge to wear on his cap. TROIANI COLLECTION.

Regulation U.S. red morocco belt with three embossed gilt stripes, worn by Maj. Gen. Amos B. Eaton, commander of the Subsistence Department during the war. TROIANI COLLECTION.

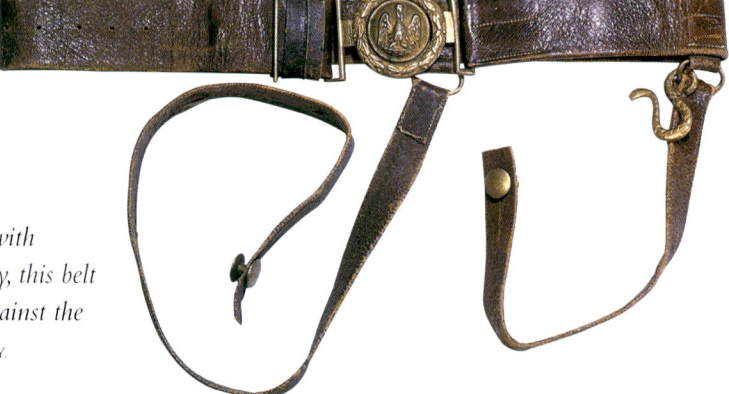

An unusual Louisiana red morocco leather officer's belt with interlocking state seal buckle. Of particularly high quality, this belt features a snake device sword hook to carry the sword against the hip when walking on foot. MUSEUM OF CONNECTICUT HISTORY.

^{1}/2-inch dark blue stripes.[3] It is evident from the lack of surviving examples and contemporary photographs that this regulation was not at all popular and was often ignored in favor of the standard dark blue frock coat.

The organization of the U.S. Army in 1861 made allowance for enlisted men in only the Medical Department, the Corps of Engineers, the Corps of Topographical Engineers, and the Ordnance Department. The other special branches were composed of officers only.[4] These officers wore the same regulation uniforms as officers of the other branches of the army, with the exception of appropriate insignia on the hat and a dark blue background on the shoulder strap. For full dress occasions, they wore epaulets that included, along with the insignia of rank, an additional device that indicated the corps or department in which they served.[5]

Confederate regulations of 1861 dictated that the uniforms of general officers, as well as officers of the Adjutant General's, Quartermaster, and Commissary General's Departments, and corps of engineers, have buff facings on the collars and cuffs, and that medical officers' uniforms be trimmed with black.[6] All of these officers were to wear dark blue trousers and caps.[7] As with most Confederate officers' uniforms, these regulations were not always strictly adhered to. Confederate enlisted men assigned to the various staff departments were generally detached from various combat regiments and always continued to wear the uniform of their original service. With Confederate uniforms, particularly those worn by persons in high command, while regulations set a standard, reality was often something quite different. The dictates of availability and of personal taste often superseded everything else.

Within both the Union and Confederate armies, the expanded duties brought on by the war meant a rapid expansion of all special branches. The need for rapid communications in the field brought hundreds of officers and enlisted men into the Signal Corps. Although not strictly a separate branch, the development of organized pioneers at various levels of command served to set these men apart from their comrades in the infantry or cavalry. Both signalmen and pioneers were usually detached from line combat regiments and wore regulation army uniforms distinguished only by sleeve insignia indicative of their special skills. The 1864 quartermaster's manual described the pioneer insignia as two crossed hatchets of cloth the same color as the trim of the uniform, to be worn on each arm above the elbow. Each hatchet was 5^1/2 inches long, with the blade 2 inches long. A corporal was to wear the crossed hatchets above and resting on the chevron. By 1864, signalmen had been authorized to wear embroidered signal flags on each sleeve in a manner similar to the hatchets of the pioneers. Hospital stewards also wore distinctive sleeve insignia: a 1^3/4-inch-wide half chevron of emerald green cloth, to be worn on the sleeve angled down, with an embroidered caduceus of yellow silk 2 inches long in the center.

Within the special branches of both the Union and Confederate armies, a multitude of civilian employees served in the offices in the capital cities and at the various depots. These men and women dealt with the mountains of paperwork necessary to keep armies in the field, although the men constituted a reserve pool of potential combat soldiers that could be used in an emergency. On May 30, 1863, Maj.

Pair of embroidered shoulder straps owned by Col. John Wilson of the 43rd New York Volunteers at the time of his death in the battle of the Wilderness on May 6, 1864. This set is still with the original pasteboard box bearing the label of Tiffany & Co., one of the ultimate military outfitters of the day. COLLECTION OF NEW YORK STATE DIVISION OF MILITARY AND NAVAL AFFAIRS.

William S. Downer, superintendent of armories in Richmond, received an order from the office of the chief of ordnance to organize "all able bodied men under [his] charge, including the clerks, into companies of not less than 60 or more than 80 men. . . . Uniforms to consist of pantaloons and shirt, will be made of blue serge—shirt trimmed with red."[8] The following year, the clerks in the Quartermaster Department in Washington and the major U.S. supply depot of Nashville were organized into battalions called Quartermaster Volunteers. These men received standard Federal uniforms of fatigue blouses, forage caps, and trousers. In both cases, the services of these civilian soldiers would be required. Those in Washington manned the city's defenses in July during Confederate general Jubal Early's advance to the northern defenses of the capital. In December 1864, at the battle of Nashville, the Quartermaster Volunteers were called on to aid in the repulse of the Confederate attack.

General officers in both the Union and Confederate armies wore uniforms that were intended to make them readily recognizable by those who would have a need to approach them or to receive direct commands from them. These marks of superior rank at times also made their position of authority apparent from a distance to enemy sharpshooters or even individual soldiers during close combat. The result is apparent from the number of generals on both sides killed and

Federal officer's regulation "cloak coat" worn by Col. Ezra Carmen of the 13th New Jersey Volunteers. This opulent, French-inspired overcoat for officers featured a detachable cape that could be used with the overcoat or independently. The wearer's rank was indicated by a varying number of flat, black silk braided knots at the cuff. TROIANI COLLECTION.

wounded during the war. At the battle of Spotsylvania on May 9, 1864, Gen. John Sedgwick, commanding the Union VI Army Corps, was killed by a Confederate sharpshooter. Two days later, the renowned Confederate cavalry commander J. E. B. Stuart was mortally wounded by a dismounted Federal cavalryman in the fight at Yellow Tavern, Virginia. It is likely that those who fired the fatal shots knew only that the uniforms of their targets were those of enemy commanders.

UNITED STATES

U.S. Army regulations of 1861 were specific in describing the uniform of general officers. Nevertheless, generals were prone to embellish and alter their uniforms. For every rule set down, there is at least one exception.[9]

Headgear
The regulations of 1861 refer to both a hat and cap for generals. The new hat was of a pattern commonly referred to as the Hardee hat. The shape was identical to that prescribed for enlisted men, but the officer's hat was of a finer quality, and rather than a wool hat cord, it had a gold cord with acorn-shaped ends. The insignia on the front of both the hat and cap was a gold embroidered "US" surrounded by a wreath of like material. Several variations of the 1858 forage cap were favored by officers. Generals' caps were embellished with a band of dark blue velvet toward the lower edge. All of this aside, photographic evidence shows that most generals, and indeed most officers, preferred the slouch hat for wear in the field.

Coats
All officers of the U.S. Army were mandated to wear dark blue frock coats. Those ranking above captain were to have a double-breasted coat with two rows of buttons. It was possible to determine at a glance that the wearer was a general by a quick look at the placement of the buttons. A major general was to have nine in each row, placed by threes, while a brigadier general was to have two rows of eight, placed by

twos. For generals, the collars and cuffs of the coats were to be of dark blue velvet.

As the war progressed, so did the popularity of the looser-fitting sack coat for undress. Numerous examples of this coat can be found in photographs and museum collections. It was normal for those worn by generals to maintain the style of the frock coat with regard to button placement, with the coat being of a much more relaxed, and therefore more comfortable, cut.

Trousers
Trousers of generals and staff officers were to be dark blue. Generals had no stripe, welt, or cord down the outer seam. Staff officers by regulation had a seam welt of gold color.

Insignia of Rank
Shoulder straps indicated rank with silver stars placed on a dark blue background. A major general commanding an army was allowed to wear straps with three stars, while the normal straps for a man of that rank would have two stars. A brigadier general's straps would have a single star.

Sash
Generals were allowed to wear a buff-colored silk sash, while all other officers wore a sash of crimson silk. When a general was on duty in the field, his sash was often stored with his baggage.

Sword Belt
The belt from which an officer's sword was suspended was worn over the sash. For officers other than generals, the belt and slings were of black leather. Generals were authorized a belt of Russian leather, with three stripes of gold embroidery around the belt and similar embroidery on the slings.

Boots
Although the regulations called only for an ankle, or Jefferson, boot for all officers, most generals, particularly those with the army in the field, wore boots that extended well up the leg. The style and cut of these varied with the taste of the wearer.

CONFEDERATE STATES

The uniform for Confederate general officers was set down in the regulations established for the Confederate army June 6, 1861, in War Department General Order No. 9. It is inter-

General's regulation kepi with dark blue velvet band and embroidered staff wreath on the front. This cap belonged to Maj. Gen. Amos B. Eaton, commissary general of the U.S. Army. TROIANI COLLECTION.

esting to note that the insignia of rank for Confederate generals was patterned after those of the Austrian and French Armies.[10]

Headgear

As with the Federal army, Confederate general officers were authorized to wear a variety of headgear. General Lee was often described as wearing a black or tan slouch hat, but during the Gettysburg campaign of 1863, an eyewitness noted that he was wearing a "broad brimmed straw hat."[11] Some Confederate generals also favored kepis or forage caps, usually adorning them with four parallel strands of gold braid extending from the band on all four sides and intertwined on the top. Gen. George E. Pickett wore such a cap at Gettysburg. Most generals owned several different pieces of headgear, with the style, type, and color worn on any particular occasion solely at the discretion of the general himself.[12]

Coat

In similar fashion to their Union counterparts, Confederate generals owned, and wore at their discretion, both the frock coat and sack coat. Although some color variations existed, these coats were in most cases made of any number of shades of gray wool, depending on the available material. The collar and cuffs of the frock coat were faced with buff-colored material.[13] Rather than shoulder straps, as worn in the Federal army, the insignia of rank for a Confederate officer was sewn on the standing collar of the frock coat or on the fold-over collar of the sack coat. Confederate generals were further distinguished by four parallel strands of gold braid on both sleeves of the frock coat, which intertwined in a distinctive loop pattern and extended from the cuff to the elbow. Some Confederate generals had made and wore a waist-length jacket cut in a similar pattern to the frock coat, without the tails.

Trousers

Confederate regulations called for general officers to wear dark blue trousers with a double row of gold braid on each leg. While these were certainly worn, it is likely that gray trousers matching the coat were more common attire. Rather than the double row of braid, many wore a simple welt of white or buff cord inset in the outer seam of the trousers, and some preferred to have neither stripe nor welt, as in the Federal army.[14]

Insignia of Rank

Confederate insignia of rank was based on that of both the Austrians and the French. The sleeve braid was unmistakably French, while the rank designation worn on the collar of all Confederate officers was heavily influenced by that of the Austrian Army. Generals of all grades wore a grouping of three stars within a wreath, the center star being larger. Portraits of Gen. Robert E. Lee show him with three stars with no wreath, but he was the exception. Lee was also known to shun most trappings of rank, including sleeve braid, and rarely even carried a sword.

Sash

The buff sash that was authorized for Federal generals was also designated for those serving the Confederacy.

Sword Belt

Here, too, Confederate regulations followed those of the United States. General officers' belts were to be of "Russian leather with three stripes of gold embroidery; the slings embroidered on both sides." A belt very closely following this pattern, with a finely cast Arkansas belt plate, was worn by Gen. Patrick R. Cleburne.[15] It is likely that other Confederate generals wore similar belts, with plates proclaiming their state heritage. Buckles of the circular, two-piece, interlocking type were used extensively by Confederate officers. At least one photograph of Robert E. Lee shows him with this type of buckle on a belt that follows the pattern described in the regulations.[16] Other photographs of Lee, as well as other Confederate generals, show clearly that a plain black leather belt was often worn by those in command.

Boots

In the field, most, if not all, Confederate generals wore boots. The variety and style were dictated only by the taste of the wearer and the availability of the type of boot he preferred.

Topographical engineers were responsible for producing accurate maps for the army. In March 1863, the topographical engineers were absorbed by the larger Corps of Engineers, and the distinctive "TE" and shield insignia seen on these epaulets were dropped from service. WEST POINT MUSEUM.

CONFEDERATE GENERAL BRAXTON BRAGG

The detractors of Confederate general Braxton Bragg found him uncouth, judgmental, psychotic, tyrannical, incompetent, quarrelsome, vindictive, and lacking in personal skills. His admirers, on the other hand, thought him brave, genial, generous, witty, intellectual, a good subordinate, untiring in his work, and an outstanding Regular army officer whose talent for organization, training, and discipline was exemplary.

Forty-five-year-old Braxton Bragg was given the rank of full general of the Confederate army on August 6, 1862. This was an honor shared by only five others: Robert E. Lee, Albert Sidney Johnston, Joseph E. Johnston, Samuel Cooper, and Pierre G. T. Beauregard. Quite a promotion for a man said to be responsible in great part for the Confederate defeat in the West!

Physically, Bragg was described as "a tall, slim man, with a small round head covered in gray f[r]izzly hair." To many observers, he often appeared "pale and careworn." Bragg suffered many ailments, ranging from migraine headaches to rheumatism to possibly malaria. Symptoms of these illnesses were aggravated by the tremendous stress he felt as an army commander. To protect his head from the sun, Bragg often wore a white havelock, "which rendered [his countenance] even more haggard," said one casual observer.

Photographs of Braxton Bragg show that, being the Regular army officer that he was, he followed the Confederate uniform regulations to the letter. As general, he wore a tunic of fine gray cloth, his rank shown by two rows of buttons on the breast, eight in each row, placed in pairs. On his sleeves were sewn four strands of $1/8$-inch-wide gold braid, extending around the cuff and up the outside of the sleeve to the elbow. The collar, cuff, and tunic edge piping were of buff cloth. On the tunic collar, Bragg's rank insignia consisted of a wreath around three small, embroidered gold stars. The center star was $1 1/4$ inches in diameter, the others only $3/4$ inch. Bragg's trousers were of dark blue wool, with two stripes of gold lace, $5/8$ inch wide and $1/8$ inch apart, at the seam. A sash of buff silk, with silk bullion fringe, was worn under a sword belt of Russian leather, ornamented with three stripes of gold embroidery.

In a full standing photo of Bragg, he wears the red sash of a staff officer and the presentation sword and belt given to him by the citizens of Mobile for his outstanding service in the Mexican War of 1847. Buff leather gauntlets, Jefferson (ankle) boots, and a dark blue cloth cap, ornamented with four gold braids and covered with a white havelock, complete Bragg's uniform.

As commanding general of the Army of Tennessee in the West from December 1862 to December 1863, Bragg had

become a scapegoat for many of the army's losses and failures. Some researchers believe that Bragg's full story is not yet told—that the present generation of Civil War historians in their passion have yet to do him justice. The great rectifiers, time and historical research, will be on Bragg's side.

Bragg himself had strong feelings about what would hasten the defeat of the Confederacy. In a letter to his wife, written on April 8, 1862, just two days after the battle of Shiloh, Bragg declared, "If we fail, it is our own fault!" He went on to say that universal suffrage, politics, furloughs, and whiskey would destroy their chances.

Regulation Confederate general's coat worn by Thomas Lafayette Rosser. It was captured from his headquarters wagon in the Shenandoah Valley by his West Point classmate and old friend George Armstrong Custer. Custer, ever the prankster, left a note for Rosser saying that in the future, the coats would fit better if made "a trifle shorter in the tails." WEST POINT MUSEUM.

MARGUERITE MERINGTON, *THE CUSTER STORY* (NEW YORK: DEVIN-ADAIR, 1950), 128.

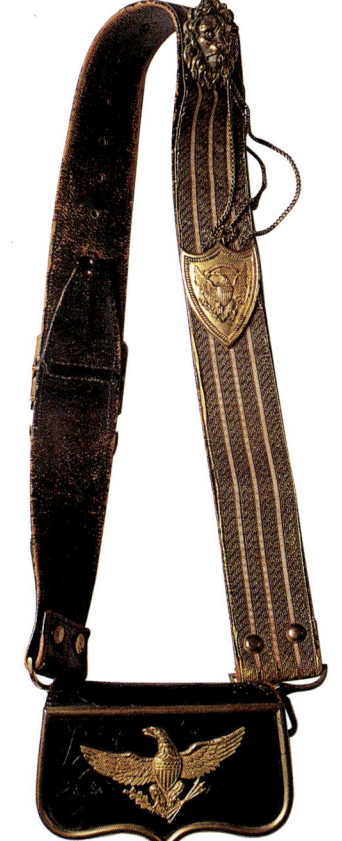

Described in the Schuyler, Hartley & Graham goods catalog as "gold and Silk Belt and Cartridge box for Staff Officers," a more useless accoutrement could not have existed. Notwithstanding, they were periodically worn in the field, and indeed, flamboyant Col. Thomas Francis Meagher of the Irish Brigade wore his during the battle of Antietam. A clone of its French prototype, this sumptuous specimen belonged to Silas P. Richmond, colonel of the 3rd Massachusetts Volunteer Infantry and aide-de-camp to Gen. Benjamin Butler. TROIANI COLLECTION.

Coat worn by Gen. Franklin Gardner, who commanded the Confederate garrison at the siege of Port Hudson in 1863. Aside from the four simple gold chevrons on the sleeves, this coat complies with the regulations for generals. Branch color for general staff often ran the gamut from yellowish buff to pure white. CONFEDERATE MEMORIAL HALL, CLAUDE LEVET PHOTOGRAPH.

Confederate officer's belt with interlocking tongue and wreath "CS" brass buckle, worn by Brig. Gen. James Holt Clanton. Elected colonel of the 1st Alabama Cavalry in 1861, Clanton served through the war until wounded at Bluff Spring, Florida, in 1865.

COLLECTION OF NEW YORK STATE DIVISION OF MILITARY & NAVAL AFFAIRS.

GENERALS ROBERT E. LEE AND A. P. HILL, GETTYSBURG CAMPAIGN, 1863

The Confederate army that marched north into Pennsylvania in June 1863 was full of confidence and hope. At their head rode a man who, for many, had become a living legend—Robert E. Lee. With him was one of his most trusted lieutenants, Ambrose Powell Hill, commanding the Army of Northern Virginia's newly formed III Corps.

The uniforms worn by these men during the fateful days of this campaign were in a measure indicative of the self-confidence earned by two years of war. Those who saw General Lee invariably commented on his well-groomed, neat appearance. As he had his personal baggage with him, many daily clothing options were at his disposal. One staff officer, G. Moxley Sorrell, observed that Lee rarely carried a sword but always had his binoculars by his side. On the march during the Gettysburg campaign, a soldier of the 17th Mississippi remembered that "he wore a long linen duster which so enveloped his uniform as to make it invisible." The image was further enhanced by a "broad brimmed straw hat, evidently the art of his many lady admirers." An account in the *Harrisburg Daily Patriot* described him as wearing "a heavy overcoat with a large cape and a black felt hat." Another witness quoted in *Gettysburg Sources,* commented that on July 1 he was "plain and neat in his uniform of gray. Hat of gray felt with medium brim and boots fitted neatly coming to his knee with a border of fair leather an inch wide." Lee's unadorned style was perhaps more of a surprise to those who were not close to him, or

DICK AND M. E. CLOW

even in the same army. Hospital Steward Henry F. Miller, Company D, 142nd Pennsylvania Volunteers, while attending wounded behind Confederate lines at Gettysburg on July 3, 1863, wrote in his diary that "General Lee and several of his Staff Officers were in the Hospital this morning. Lee was dressed like a citizen without any side arms." Lt. Col. Arthur J. L. Fremantle commented of Lee at Gettysburg, "he generally wears a long grey jacket, a high black felt hat, and blue trousers tucked into his Wellington boots. I never saw him

carry arms; and the only mark of his military rank are the three stars on his collar." Contradicting others about the sword, Gen. John Bell Hood reminisced about Lee on the morning of July 2, "General Lee with his coat buttoned to throat, sabre belt around his waist and field glasses pending at his side walked up and down in the shade of large trees near us." Lt. J. Winder Laird who saw the great commander nearly a year later, remarked in his diary on the general's plain dress and noted that while mounted, "he carried a bush in his

Confederate staff officer's kepi worn by Maj. Hugh Mortimer Nelson while serving on the staff of Gen. Richard Ewell in 1862. Rather than the more customary quatrefoil configuration of gold lace on the crown, three concentric rings of gold tape were used. TROIANI COLLECTION.

Staff officer's frock coat worn by Capt. Edward C. Wharton as quartermaster general in Houston, Texas, from 1861 to 1865. As per Confederate States regulations, the coat is faced in buff, the designating color for a staff officer. GARY HENDERSHOTT.

Straw cap worn by Confederate general Pierre Gustave Toutant Beauregard during the war. With a black velvet band and stars proclaiming his rank, such a lightweight cap would have proved most acceptable in the heat of the South. Beauregard is recorded as having worn a straw hat at the battle of First Manassas.

CONFEDERATE MEMORIAL HALL, CLAUDE LEVET PHOTOGRAPH.

hand with which he brushed flies from his horse."

One of Lee's most able subordinates, Gen. Ambrose Powell Hill, has been inaccurately characterized by modern writers as invariably wearing a bright red battle shirt throughout the entire war. It has been noted that General Hill, in the heat of the summer during the 1862 Peninsula campaign, sometimes wore a red and black striped shirt, and when on the march, an unadorned "hunting shirt" without insignia of rank. However, the uniform he wore more often on campaign, "a Fatigue jacket of gray flannel, his felt hat slouched over his noble brow" and hip-length boots, must certainly have seemed more appropriate attire. In the battle that surely lay ahead, the officer's sack coat, with general's rank plainly visible, would forestall any question of authority. This could be particularly important when commanding troops in the newly formed corps—troops who may not yet know him on sight. In addition, unlike General Lee, and perhaps some other Army of Northern Virginia officers, according to British military observer Lt. Col. Arthur J. L. Fremantle, General Hill most always wore his sword.

BERDAN'S SHARPSHOOTERS

STEVEN ROGERS

In the fall of 1861, a unique regiment of men was being raised throughout several Northern states, from New England to Wisconsin. Those members encamped at Weehawken, New Jersey, were described as having the "complete outfit of the Sharpshooters, which consists of a regulation undress blue jacket and Austrian gray pants, a frock coat and fatigue cap of green cloth, an extra felt hat with leather visor and cape, blankets, shoes underclothes, etc." Col. Hiram Berdan ultimately recruited eighteen companies of proven riflemen for the defense of the Union, and two regiments were formed from them: the lst and 2nd Regiments of U.S. Sharpshooters. Berdan was a mechanical engineer from New York City who was also one of the top amateur marksmen in the United States prior to the war. He hoped to prove the value of such men in war and to promote his ideas and inventions in the process

It was Berdan's idea to clothe his men in distinctive uniforms. Originally he had even proposed a fringed blue sack

Silver III Army Corps badge with red enameled center, inscribed to an unknown soldier of Company H, 2nd U.S. Sharpshooters. TROIANI COLLECTION.

Forest green regulation frock coat worn by Sgt. William F. Tilson of the 2nd U.S. Sharpshooters (Berdan's). Manufactured at Schuylkill Arsenal in Philadelphia, the green cloth was made by redyeing standard dark blue to the desired hue. The chevrons, which were privately purchased from sutlers, are of deep green velvet. Unique to sharpshooter units, the buttons were made of black hard rubber. Tilson served for the entire war and was wounded nine times until the loss of a foot at Petersburg concluded his military career. TROIANI COLLECTION.

coat and winter uniform of gray, but the Sharpshooters, as they became known, did indeed wear an unusual uniform. Their uniform or frock coats were styled exactly as the Federal pattern 1858 coats, but were of dark green with emerald or medium green trim on collar and cuffs. Their trousers, first of light blue, were eventually of dark green as well. More distinctive, however, was the gray felt havelock hat. A patent waterproof headgear, it was accompanied initially with a seamless waterproof gray felt overcoat, edged with green. Both of these items proved of limited value, the overcoats becoming stiff when wet, and both items being too "secessionist" in color to be safely worn at the battlefront. Other unusual clothing included russet leather leggings, originally made by a New York firm for $2.25 a pair. The regimental knapsacks, ordered from "Messrs. Tiffany" of New York City, were of "the hide Knapsack, Prussian Pattern," and cost $3.75 each. An idea of what was required to clothe the 1st and 2nd Regiments of Sharpshooters can be gained from a list of articles sent to Washington for distribution on November 12, 1861:

1000 prs. Sky blue trousers
1600 prs. Leggins
1100 Ostrich feathers

1000 Privts. Green trousers
  32 Sgts Green chevrons
   2 Sergt. Maj. Green chevrons
   2 Q.M. Sergt. Chevrons Green
   2 Commy. Sergt. Chevrons Green
  32 Green cords & tassels for bugles
 400 Gt. Coats, seamless, green trimmings
 500 Knapsacks, similar to those furnished to this corps

The ostrich feathers were not to trim uniform or Hardee hats, as might be expected, but were worn on the fronts of the green forage caps. Bugles were used instead of drums to sound calls for the "chippies," as the Sharpshooters were nicknamed by the soldiers of the 14th Brooklyn because of their use of bugles for reveille.

Berdan wanted his men armed with the new M1859 Sharps breech-loading rifles. Instead, in addition to their privately owned target rifles, the initial issue to the regiments was Colt revolving rifles. Eventually, after a near mutiny in the 1st Regiment, the regiments received Sharps rifles, which they carried and used with great effect through the war. Green coats and Sharps rifles became trademarks of the Sharpshooters, but it was their gallant service through the war that made them a Civil War legend.

CONFEDERATE STATES MARINE CORPS

The Confederate States Marine Corps was, in almost all respects, a duplicate of the United States Marine Corps, and its functions were similar. Confederate States marines saw action in nearly every major engagement on the South Atlantic and Gulf coasts. Most of the ironclad rams carried marine detachments, as did all but one of the Confederate commerce raiders. Battle honors included the engagement at Ship Island, Mississippi, July 9, 1861; raid on Santa Rosa Island, Florida, October 8–9, 1861; engagement at Head of the Passes, Louisiana, October 12, 1861; battle of Port Royal, South Carolina, November 7, 1861; bombardment of Fort Pickens, Florida, November 22–24, 1861; battle of Hampton Roads, Virginia, March 8–9, 1862; battle of New Orleans, April 24, 1862; battle of First Drewry's Bluff, May 15, 1862; battle of Fort Sumter, South Carolina, September 8–9, 1863; destruction of USS *Underwriter* off New Berne, North Carolina, February 1, 1864; battle of Second Drewry's Bluff, May 9–16, 1864; capture of USS *Water Witch* in Ossabaw Sound, Georgia, June 3, 1864; battle of Mobile Bay and Fort Gaines, Alabama, August 5–8, 1864; siege of Savannah, December 10–21, 1864; battles of Fort Fisher, North Carolina, December 23–25, 1864, and January 13–15, 1865; battle of Sayler's Creek, Virginia, April 6, 1865; and the siege and battle of Fort Blakely, Alabama, April 2–9, 1865. The last Marines to lay down their arms did so just north of Mobile, Alabama, May 10, 1865.

The arms and accoutrements of Confederate States marines varied from post to post. Long arms included the .69-caliber M1822 musket, altered from flintlock to percussion; the M1861 Springfield .58-caliber rifle musket; the Austrian Lorenz .58-caliber rifle musket; and the prized .577-caliber Enfield rifle musket and rifle.

The field or sea service kit was patterned on those worn in the British service. The cartridge box, cap pouch, and bayonet were intended to be worn on the waist belt, but cartridge boxes were also attached to a separate leather shoulder belt. The knapsack was attached to the waist belt by means of metal slides. A haversack and canteen were slung over the shoulder. All leather components of the kit were black. Plates of undetermined design for the waist belt and cartridge box were a regular issue.

No uniform regulations for the Confederate States Marine Corps have ever been located, and given the many changes that occurred during the course of the war, it is likely that none were ever officially ordered.

In 1861, marine officers lately resigned from the U.S. Marine Corps wore the uniforms from the old service. Newly commissioned officers were obliged to purchase their uniforms. In late 1861, marine officers were wearing gray uniform coats with navy blue collars and cuffs. It appears that the buttons were not standardized. Some officers wore state seal buttons. Army-style rank devices were worn on the collars. Navy blue trousers and kepis rounded out the uniforms. Sidearms were privately purchased or bought from government stores. Later, the sleeve braid worn by army officers was attached to the sleeves of the marine officers' uniform coats, which still had the navy blue collars and cuffs. The navy blue of the trousers was changed to gray, with a navy blue stripe attached to the outside seam. In 1863, Russian-style shoulder knots, identical to those worn by officers of the U.S. Marine Corps, became part of the officers' uniforms.

Uniforms for enlisted Confederate marines initially came from Federal stores captured at Pensacola, Florida. The first regular issue of uniforms, in September and October 1861, consisted of navy blue satinette frock coats and jean trousers. Later, gray uniforms from the C.S. Army Quartermaster Department were issued, adapted to marine usage by the addition of navy blue trim on the cuffs, front, and collar. Gray kepis with a navy blue branch band completed the assemblage.

White linen trousers and overalls were summer issue for the enlisted men, tweed greatcoats were issued during the winter months, and blue fatigue jackets were worn year-round. The uniform button initially had a Roman "M" later replaced by the button of the artillery, with a Roman "A." Evidence exists that a distinguishing mark was worn on the kepi—the hunting horn and Old English "M" of the U.S. Marine Corps.

Ambulance Corps forage cap with designating green band 1 1/4 inches wide, as authorized in August 1863, superseding the previously 2-inch-wide band.

TROIANI COLLECTION.

GENERAL ORDER NO. 85, ARMY OF THE POTOMAC.

UNITED STATES MARINES, 1861–65

In January 1861, the officers and rank and file of the United States Marine Corps numbered less than 2,000, more than half of those attached to warships of the U.S. Navy. Four years later, there were twice that number, serving ashore and afloat in approximately the same proportions.

At the battle of Bull Run on July 21, 1861, a battalion of some 350 marines, most in the service less than six weeks, engaged the Confederates three times in the seesaw fighting on Henry Hill. It was they who made the penetration of Rebel lines while supporting the attack of the 14th Brooklyn.

Aboard ship, marines, manning main or secondary batteries, won praise for their gallantry in action at the battles of New Orleans, April 24, 1861; Hampton Roads, March 8–9, 1862; First Drewry's Bluff, May 15, 1862; Mobile Bay, August 5, 1864; and First Fort Fisher, December 23–25, 1864.

The uniform worn by the U.S. Marines during the Civil War was ordained by the regulations approved by the Navy Department on January 24, 1859. It was not until the middle of 1861, however, that all marines then in service were outfitted with the new uniform.

The full dress uniform of the marine officer consisted of a dark blue, double-breasted frock coat with a high standing collar with two loops of gold lace on each side. Sky blue trousers were worn during the winter months and white linen during the summer months. (Staff officers and officers serving at sea could wear dark blue trousers.) Rank was indicated by loops of gold lace on the cuff and by army-style devices mounted on gold epaulets. A scarlet welt was sewn into the outer seam of the trousers. Headgear for staff and field-grade officers was a French chapeau with red feather adornment; for company-grade officers, it was a stiff black uniform cap with a gold net pom-pom (later changed to red feathers) at the front top and a gilt U.S. shield with the

marine hunting horn emblem and half wreath in the front center.

The undress uniform worn by marine officers consisted of a dark blue, double-breasted frock coat with a short stand-up collar, and the same trousers worn with the full dress uniform. During the summer months, a uniform of white linen, cut in the same fashion, was worn. Rank was indicated by army rank devices mounted on gold Russian shoulder knots with a scarlet underlining. In 1863, an order did away with shoulder knots for field-grade and staff officers, authorizing them to wear army-style shoulder straps. A dark blue cloth fatigue hat (French kepi style) with a band of black silk at the base of the crown was worn with the undress uniform. Slim bands of black ribbed silk were sewn vertically into the sides of the kepi and looped to a quatrefoil knot in the crown. The cap ornament was a gold embroidered bugle on a scarlet background, with a silver, Old English "M" in the center of the ring of the bugle. In summer months, a flat-crowned straw hat with a black band at its base was worn.

Marine officers wore a dark blue fatigue jacket cut short at the waist, with sixteen small marine buttons aligned in the center. The collar was edged with gold lace, and a six-inch inverted V made from this same gold lace adorned each sleeve. Shoulder knots were worn with the fatigue jacket. The overcoat for marine officers was of dark blue cloth, fastened by four frog buttons, with rank indicated by the number of braids in the knot at the cuff of the sleeves.

The 1859 regulations replaced the M1827 Mameluke sword with the M1850 army foot officer's sword. The sword belt was white glazed leather and fastened by the M1851 eagle-wreath sword belt plate. A sash of crimson silk net was worn under the sword belt.

The full dress uniform for enlisted marines consisted of a dark blue, double-breasted frock coat with a high standing collar adorned with a horizontal double row of yellow worsted lace. Brass epaulets were worn on the shoulders, with yellow worsted bullion of varying widths according to rank. Sky blue woolen trousers were worn during the winter months, and white linen during the summer months. The sergeant major, quartermaster sergeant, and all musicians had a scarlet cord sewn into the outer seam of the trouser legs. The dress hat was a dark blue shako, with a brass U.S. shield with the marine ornament in the center, and a half wreath identical to that worn by marine officers. A red pom-pom was worn on the front center of the hat. Noncommissioned officers wore red worsted sashes. Stripes made of yellow lace on a red background were attached, points up, above the elbow on the sleeves of their coats to denote rank. Noncommissioned officers were authorized to wear the M1850 foot officer's sword, but on a sliding frog attached to the waist belt.

Wool felt and leather uniform cap of the U.S. Marines as specified in the regulations of 1859, made by the firm of Bent & Bush in Boston. This cap was seldom, if ever, used in active service, the fatigue cap, or kepi, being preferred. RAY DARIDA COLLECTION.

The enlisted undress uniform consisted of a fitted frock coat with a scarlet welt sewn into the lower seam of the short standing collar, the same trousers worn with the dress uniform, and a fatigue hat in the style of the French kepi. The marine ornament was worn on the front center of the fatigue hat. In summer months, a white linen cover was worn over the crown of the hat. Rank chevrons in the same style and color as on the dress uniform were worn on the frock coat in the same position.

Dark-blue flannel fatigue sacks, actually shirts that opened halfway down the front, were also issued to enlisted marines. These were later replaced by flannel frock coats with fold-down collars. Rank stripes were worn on both the fatigue shirts and coats.

Enlisted marines wore white cross belts—a cartridge box belt running from the left shoulder to the right hip, and a bayonet belt in opposition. An unadorned oval-shaped plate was worn on the bayonet belt at the intersection of the two belts. A white waist belt with an unadorned belt plate completed the ensemble.

For the winter months, marine enlisted men were issued overcoats of blue-gray wool with stand-up collars, buttons down the front, and detachable capes. Rank stripes were worn on the cuffs rather than in the usual place above the elbow.

One uniform item for both officers and enlisted men, basically unchanged since 1775, was the leather stock worn around the neck.

CEMETERY HILL, GETTYSBURG, JULY 1, 1863

Since early morning on July 1, 1863, a fierce and bloody battle had raged in the fields north and west of Gettysburg, Pennsylvania. For the Union army, the brunt of the fighting had fallen on the shoulders of the I and XI Corps of infantry. Now, as the tide of battle turned against them, they fell back through the town to the high ground marked by a towering brick gate that served as the entrance to the community cemetery. During the retreat through the town's streets, regiments became mixed. Now I Corps troops—the 14th Brooklyn Zouaves, wearing the distinctive jackets and red chasseur trousers, 142nd Pennsylvania Bucktails with deer tails adorning their forage caps, as well as other regiments— mingled with XI Corps soldiers, some, in regiments such as the 45th New York, in state-issue jackets. Many from both corps had chosen to fight in the four-button fatigue blouse that had become the favored campaign dress of most of the Federal army. Were it not for the newly issued corps badges— a crescent for the XI Corps and a sphere for the I Corps— there would have been little except the brass regimental numbers on their caps to tell them apart. These men would re-form under the guidance of Gen. Winfield Scott Hancock, commander of the II Corps, who had temporarily taken overall command of the field, as well as Gen. Abner Doubleday in command of the I Corps and Gen. Oliver O. Howard leading the XI Corps. Along with their comrades of the Army of the Potomac, they would emerge the victors in the battle that many believe sealed the fate of the Confederacy.

Lt. Green Smith, son of famed abolitionist Gerritt Smith, wore this black braided kepi with a staff insignia during the Petersburg campaign of 1864. The crown is emblazoned with a red anchor and cannon badge of the 1st Division, IX Army Corps. TROIANI COLLECTION.

Federal general's slouch hat with die-cut cloth badge of the 3rd Division of the III Army Corps. The all-gilt cord and acorns were specified for generals, with black and gilt for other commissioned ranks. TROIANI COLLECTION.

Regulation Federal brigadier general's coat with dark blue velvet collar and cuffs, and the buttons spaced by pairs. This coat was worn by William S. Tilton, who commanded a brigade in the Wheatfield at Gettysburg and was appointed brevet brigadier general on September 9, 1864. TROIANI COLLECTION.

Although it had been proposed earlier in the year, the badge of the X Army Corps was adopted officially on July 25, 1864. This staff red, white, and blue version was used by Lt. William H. Pierpont of the 7th Connecticut Volunteers. MUSEUM OF CONNECTICUT HISTORY.

VETERAN RESERVE CORPS, CORPORAL, 8TH REGIMENT, MARCH 1864

The Veteran Reserve Corps was instituted in April 1863 under its original designation of the Invalid Corps. The idea was an excellent one, in that it provided an opportunity for disabled U.S. soldiers to continue to serve their country even though they were no longer physically able to serve in fighting regiments. The name was changed a year later after a series of jokes, and even a popular song, alleged that this corps was a safe harbor for able-bodied malingerers to escape the danger of battle.

Eventually the Veteran Reserve Corps consisted of twenty-four regiments and a number of independent companies. They served in hospitals, as guards in prisoner-of-war camps, and in other noncombat capacities. In each case, they took the place of able-bodied soldiers, who could then be sent to the armies in the field. The 8th Regiment, along with the 15th, provided guards for Confederate prisoners being held at Camp Douglas, near Chicago.

The uniform of the Veteran Reserve Corps was identical to that of the soldiers of the Federal army serving in the combat forces, except for the jacket. The jacket was adopted in May 1863 and was described by quartermaster regulations as being "of sky blue kersey, with dark blue trimmings, cut like the jacket for cavalry, to come well down on the loins and abdomen." The jacket was actually varied from that issued to the cavalry, being about an inch longer, with shoulder loops and a slit on either side of the bottom edge. Officers were initially intended to be uniformed in a frock coat of sky blue cloth, but few of these were actually worn.

The arms of this corps initially consisted of obsolete weapons that had been turned in by the regiments serving at the front. The 8th Regiment of the Veteran Reserve Corps was first armed with imported muskets. In late 1864, these were replaced by Enfield rifle muskets.

Elegant set of cased medical staff officer's gilt epaulets bearing the crest "MS" within a wreath. These belonged to Asst. Surgeon Jeptha R. Boulware of the 177th New York Volunteer Infantry.

COLLECTION OF NEW YORK STATE DIVISION OF MILITARY AND NAVAL AFFAIRS.

WILLIAM RODEN

Union Army Surgeon, 1861–65

Medical officers at any level of service, from regiment to army corps, were considered members of the headquarters staff. As such, the uniform of a surgeon in the U.S. Army had little to distinguish it from that of any other staff officer of equivalent rank. Army regulations called for medical officers to wear a sash of "medium or emerald green."

The medical officer was also prescribed a sword of a pattern first adopted in 1840. Unlike the heavy-bladed swords carried by line officers, the medical staff sword was not designed for serious work in combat. The blade was 28 inches long but only ¾ inch wide at the hilt. A shield, cast as part of the guard, had the letters "MS" applied in Old English script.

Set of false embroidered Smith's patent shoulder straps for a Federal army surgeon, with the regulation Old English letters "MS" in the center. Medical staff officers used the staff background color of black. TROIANI COLLECTION.

Hospital steward's frock coat with distinctive sleeve insignia: "a caduceus two inches long, embroidered with yellow silk on each arm above the elbow, in the place indicated for a chevron, the head toward the outer seam of the sleeve." Although not noted in the regulations, all known examples have a green background. Privately purchased examples often tended to be more elaborate, with metallic embroidery on green velvet. Regulations specified crimson piping, but most existing examples of hospital stewards' frock coats are untrimmed. UNION DRUMMER BOY.

UNIFORM AND DRESS OF THE UNITED STATES ARMY, 1861 (WASHINGTON, D.C., 1861), 4, 6, 14.

Federal officer's black enameled waist belt, used by Surgeon Ambrose Pratt of the 22nd Connecticut Volunteers. Note the green stitching, the branch color of the Medical Service. TROIANI COLLECTION.

This same sword was also carried by officers of the Pay Department. Many medical officers chose to wear shoulder straps that denoted their rank in the usual manner but had the letters "MS," similar to the design found on the sword affixed to the middle of the strap.

As with the medical staffs of all armies in history, the job

of the army surgeon in either the Northern or Southern army during the Civil War was to attempt to save lives. Those who traveled with the armies in the field worked under conditions that favored the Grim Reaper. Disease, infection, and small-arms projectiles that shattered bones beyond any hope of repair were facts of daily life for these men.

CONFEDERATE STATES MEDICAL SERVICE

The Medical Service of the Confederate army was organized and patterned after the same service in the Federal army. Each regiment of infantry and cavalry had its own surgeon and assistant surgeon, who held the rank of major and captain, respectively. Senior ranking regimental surgeons would be assigned to brigade or division level, with added responsibility. All of these nominally were under the overall supervision of the surgeon general. While on paper this may appear to be ideal, in reality the quality of those surgeons who served the fighting men in the field varied as greatly as did the backgrounds of those whose health and well-being depended on them. Doubtless the majority of those who chose to follow the armies had good intentions. Most were given examinations to assure their expertise in their profession. But few were prepared for the challenge that lay before them. In solitary winter encampments, surgeons often were called upon to cope with disease of epidemic proportions. In a single battle, a regimental surgeon could well face more serious injuries than he might see in a decade or more of ordinary domestic practice.

The uniform of the Confederate surgeon was identical to that of line officers, except that the trim of the coat collar, cuffs, and trouser stripe were black, and the letters "MS" were embroidered in gold on the front of the hat or cap. Enlisted men serving with the Medical Service were usually chosen from the ranks of the various regiments and often were members of the regimental band. No distinctive uniform was issued. The nature of the work performed by those men, though not without danger, was attractive for some, who would fall out of ranks during battle to help wounded to the rear, thereby avoiding combat. To counter this, a more regulated Ambulance Corps was formed, to which men who were unfit for battle were assigned. Although not universally adopted, many enlisted men serving with the Medical Service wore red badges on their hats to set them apart from those who might have less than honor-

GREENSBORO HISTORICAL MUSEUM

able intentions. Lt. Col. Arthur J. L. Fremantle, a British observer with the Army of Northern Virginia, who described Semmes's and Barksdale's Brigades on the march during the Gettysburg campaign, took particular note of the Ambulance Corps: "In the rear of each regiment were from twenty to thirty negro slaves, and a certain number of unarmed men carrying stretchers and wearing in their hats the red badges of the ambulance corps—this an excellent institution, for it prevents unwounded men from falling out on pretense of taking wounded to the rear."

Badges for corps staff were required to be in the colors of all the divisions of that corps, usually red, white, and blue. Capt. Elliot C. Pierce of the 13th Massachusetts Volunteers wore this cap with a tricolored sphere while commanding the ambulances of the I Corps at Gettysburg. TROIANI COLLECTION.

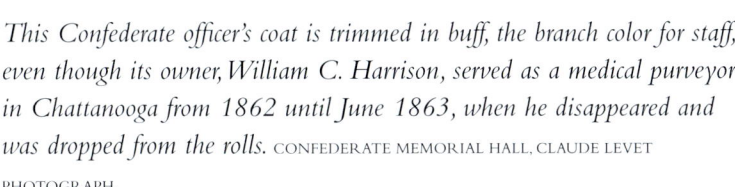

This Confederate officer's coat is trimmed in buff, the branch color for staff, even though its owner, William C. Harrison, served as a medical purveyor in Chattanooga from 1862 until June 1863, when he disappeared and was dropped from the rolls. CONFEDERATE MEMORIAL HALL, CLAUDE LEVET PHOTOGRAPH.

This sober Confederate officer's blue-gray frock coat with Federal eagle staff buttons was worn by Lt. Col. Minor Meriwether, who served as an engineer officer constructing fortifications and railroads throughout the Deep South. Meriwether's wife, Elizabeth, made the coat for him in 1862 by altering a gray civilian coat and had a jeweler cut out the collar stars from silver quarters. He wore it until his surrender with Gen. Richard Taylor in 1865. M. CUNNINGHAM COLLECTION.

ELIZABETH A. MERIWETHER, *RECOLLECTIONS OF NINETY-TWO YEARS, 1824–1916* (NASHVILLE: TENNESSEE HISTORICAL COMMISSION, 1958).

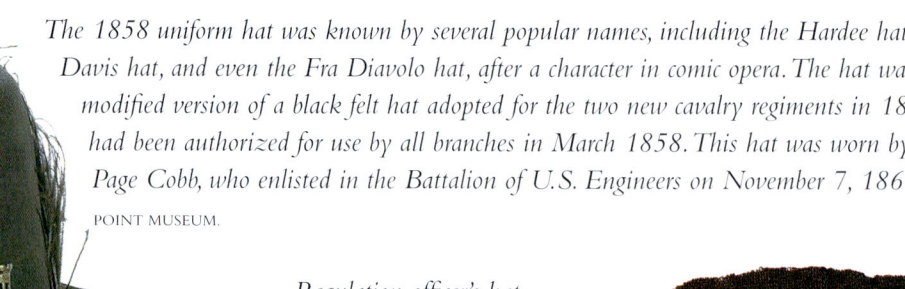

The 1858 uniform hat was known by several popular names, including the Hardee hat, the Jeff Davis hat, and even the Fra Diavolo hat, after a character in comic opera. The hat was a modified version of a black felt hat adopted for the two new cavalry regiments in 1855, and it had been authorized for use by all branches in March 1858. This hat was worn by Harlan Page Cobb, who enlisted in the Battalion of U.S. Engineers on November 7, 1861. WEST POINT MUSEUM.

Regulation officer's hat insignia of Lt. Charles B. Norton of the 50th New York Engineers, with the prescribed crest of a silver castle encompassed by gold-embroidered palm and laurel leaves. TROIANI COLLECTION.

Black sash for a Federal chaplain. Although regulations specified that all staff officers wear crimson silk net sashes, some private military goods firms, such as Schuyler, Hartley & Graham, offered black in their 1864 catalog. MUSEUM OF CONNECTICUT HISTORY.

Fatigue blouse of Maj. Gen. Nathaniel P. Banks, who commanded Union forces at the battles of Cedar Mountain and Port Hudson, and the ill-fated Red River campaign. This is a simplified version of the regulation frock coat, with less chest padding, a lay-down or stand-up collar, exterior breast pocket, and plain cuffs. TROIANI COLLECTION.

Painted wooden drum with device of Company C, 1st New York Volunteer Engineers. Like their Regular army counterparts, volunteers often used the traditional castle device. TROIANI COLLECTION.

PIONEER, ARMY OF THE CUMBERLAND, 1863

By the spring of 1863, the use of separate detachments of pioneers had been fully established in both the Army of the Potomac in the East and the Army of the Cumberland in the West. These soldiers were selected from the various regiments of a brigade or division and provided with the necessary tools to allow them to clear roads, throw up temporary earthworks, and other like duties. One task that called for quick action and bravery was the rapid throwing up of small breastworks, or lunettes, to protect artillery pieces being placed in position during battle.

As they were detached, and often worked ahead of the moving combat troops, it was necessary for pioneers to wear an identifying insignia that would clearly show that they were officially separated from their various commands. The insignia chosen was one that had been used in the Regular army since its adoption in 1851: crossed axes, each about $3\frac{1}{2}$ inches in height, cut from cloth and sewn to the sleeve of the uniform in the same position as noncommissioned officers' chevrons. These soldiers carried most of their tools—axes, picks, and spades—in leather holders attached to slings. Because these units often were in advance, and thereby exposed, positions, each man was also required to be fully armed and prepared to fight if necessary.

On May 29, 1863, a recently appointed pioneer serving in the 3rd Battalion, Pioneer Brigade, Army of the Cumberland, described his distinctive insignia and what it meant to him: "We wear a badge on our left arm. The badge has two crossed hatchets on it and that badge is the same as a pass. We can go anywhere and the guards don't trouble us any."

The pioneer chevron was worn in the U.S. Army until 1899.

Gold-braided kepi worn by Brig. Gen. John Henry Hobart Ward, who commanded a brigade of the III Army Corps at Gettysburg. Though such dress caps were occasionally worn in the field, most officers preferred a less extravagant display and wore unadorned forage caps or slouch hats. Black braid was often preferred over the eye-catching gold. GARY HENDERSHOTT.

SERGEANT OF ORDNANCE, 1863

The Ordnance Department was one of the few Special Branches that utilized both officers and enlisted men. This unique department included some of the most highly educated officers and technically competent enlisted men to serve in the U.S. Army. The deference shown to the men of Ordnance was made evident by the fact that throughout the war the enlisted men were allowed to continue to wear the dark blue trousers that by early 1863 had given way to sky blue ones in the rest of the Regular army. A letter dated February 16, 1865, from the Quartermaster General's office notes that "in the last six months . . . 396 pairs [of dark blue trousers] were for Ordnance soldiers." The same letter mentions the fact that when the change to sky-blue was ordered in 1861, the "large number of dark blue kersey trowsers [*sic*] on hand . . . were by special request, held for issue to Ordnance soldiers."

It should be noted that within the department the rank of sergeant of ordnance differed greatly from that of ordnance sergeant. Army Regulations go to great lengths to explain the unique duties and status of an ordnance sergeant. Those soldiers assigned to duty as ordnance sergeant wore a silk chevron consisting of three stripes surmounted by a large five-pointed star. They were individually posted to every fort and permanent army facility to take charge of any and all ordnance stored there. A sergeant of ordnance worked within and for the Ordnance Department and served at Ordnance facilities, such as Frankfort Arsenal, often in highly skilled positions. The rank of sergeant was usually attained within this department only after long service and proven ability.

Frankfort Arsenal was one of the main facilities for the manufacture and distribution of munitions to the army and also handled the transshipment of some arms received from major manufacturers such as Colt. Located in a northern suburb of Philadelphia the arsenal had been in existence since 1816. Senior enlisted men stationed here and at other Ordnance facilities not only supervised lower ranking enlisted workers but also filled such important positions as machinest and armorer.

Army Regulations provided a diagonal half chevron to be worn on both sleeves of the uniform coat for each five years of faithful service. Service during war was indicated by a light blue narrow stripe on each side of the chevron for artillery, and a red stripe for all other corps. With service stripes indicating over twenty years service, along with the crimson trim on his uniform and flaming bomb insignia on his hat this sergeant of ordnance would command respect on any post occupied by the U.S. Army.

One of a pair of regulation red silk tape Federal ordnance sergeant's chevrons. Although ordnance sergeants' uniforms were trimmed with crimson, regulations specified that they were "to wear the uniform of the ordnance department with the distinctive badge prescribed for the non-commissioned staff of regiments of artillery." C. PAUL LOANE COLLECTION.

REVISED UNITED STATES ARMY REGULATIONS OF 1861 (WASHINGTON, D.C.: GOVERNMENT PRINTING OFFICE, 1863), 27.

SPECIAL BRANCHES AND GENERAL OFFICERS

INTRODUCTION

1. National Archives, Record Group 109, M-331, Compiled Service Records of Confederate General and Staff Officers, file of Gen. Thomas N. Waul.
2. Ibid., Record Group 92, entry 62, vol. 22, 629; "Quartermaster's Manual of 1864" (never published, but planned for publication by Thomas Publications of Gettysburg, Pa.).
3. National Archives, Record Group 94, entry 44, 1863, General Order 158.
4. Francis B. Heitman, *Historical Register and Dictionary of the United States Army,* vol. 2 (Washington, D.C.: Government Printing Office, 1903).
5. *Regulations for the Army of the United States, 1861* (New York: Harper & Brothers, 1861); Frederick P. Todd, *American Military Equipage,* vol. 1, (Providence, R.I.: Company of Military Historians,* 1974).
6. *Regulations for the Army of the Confederate States* (Richmond, 1861).
7. Ibid.
8. National Archives, Record Group 109, M-331, Compiled Service Records of Confederate General and Staff Officers, file of William S. Downer.
9. *Regulations for the Army of the United States, 1861* (New York: Harper & Brothers, 1861); Editors of Time-Life Books, *Echoes of Glory* (Alexandria, Va.: Time-Life, 1991), Union vol., 98–102, Confederate vol., 104–7.
10. Leslie D. Jensen, *Johnny Reb: The Uniform of the Confederate Army, 1861–1865* (London: Greenhill Books, 1996).
11. Judge C. C. Cummings, "Chancellorsville, May 2, 1863," *Confederate Veteran* 23 (September 1915): 405.
12. *Echoes of Glory* Confederate vol.: 160–61.
13. Ibid., 102–7.
14. Ibid.
15. Ibid., 189.
16. William A. Turner, *Even More Confederate Faces* (Orange, Va.: Moss Publications, 1983), 150.

CONFEDERATE GENERAL BRAXTON BRAGG

Grady McWhiney, *Braxton Bragg and Confederate Defeat,* vol. 1 (New York: Columbia University Press, 1969), 269–71.

Judith Lee Hallock, *Braxton Bragg and Confederate Defeat,* vol. 2 (Tuscaloosa: University of Alabama Press, 1991), introduction.

Don C. Seitz, *Braxton Bragg: General of the Confederacy* (Columbia, S.C.: The State Company, 1924), 3, 111–12.

Grady McWhiney, "Braxton Bragg: Misplaced General," Cincinatti Civil War Rountable Presentation, n.d.

William Miller, *In Camp and Battle with the Washington Artillery of New Orleans* (Baton Rouge: Louisiana State University Press, 1966), 279.

Uniform and Dress of the Army of The Confederate States (Richmond, 1861).

GENERALS ROBERT E. LEE AND A. P. HILL, GETTYSBURG CAMPAIGN, 1863

G. Moxley Sorrell, *Recollections of a Confederate Staff Officer,* Wilmington, N.C.: Broadfoot Publishing Co., 1987), 68.

Judge C. C. Cummings, "Chancellorsville, May 2, 1863," *Confederate Veteran* 23 (September 1915): 405.

Harrisburg Daily Patriot, July 18, 1863, 1.

James Power Smith, "General Lee at Gettysburg," in *Gettysburg Sources,* compiled by James L. McLean, Jr., and Judy W. McLean (Baltimore: Butternut and Blue, 1986), 36.

Arthur J. L. Fremantle, *Three Months in the Southern States* (Edinburgh: W. Blackwood, 1863), 253–54.

I. Scheibert, "Causes of Lee's Defeat at Gettysburg," *Southern Historical Society Papers,* vol. 5 (Richmond, Va.: Southern Historical Society, 1878), 79.

Unpublished diary of Lt. J. Winder Laird, 2nd Maryland Infantry.

Lt. Gen. A. P. Hill, *Southern Historical Society Papers,* vol. 19 (Richmond, Va.: Southern Historical Society, 1891), 178.

Dr. J. William Jones, "Gen. A. P. Hill," *Confederate Veteran* 1 (August 1893): 234.

Fremantle, *Three Months in the Southern States,* 254.

BERDAN'S SHARPSHOOTERS

Charles A. Stevens, *Berdan's United States Sharpshooters in the Army of the Potomac, 1861–1865* (Dayton, Ohio: Morningside Bookshop, 1984).

New York Tribune, October 15, 1861, p. 8.

National Archives, Record Group 92, Quartermaster Letters Sent and Received, 629, 472.

CONFEDERATE STATES MARINE CORPS

Muster Rolls and Pay Rolls of Marine Detachments of the C.S. Navy, Record Group 45, entry 426, Naval Records Collection of the Office of Naval Records and Library, National Archives, Washington, D.C.

Ralph W. Donnelly, "Battle Honors and Services of Confederate Marines," *United Daughters of the Confederacy Magazine* (March 1960): 31–32.

Quarterly Returns of Ordnance and Ordnance Stores for Companies A, B, C, and E, C.S. Marine Corps, 1862–1864, Subject file of the C.S. Navy, Subject file O, "Operations of Naval Ships and Fleet Units," file OV, "Miscellaneous," Record Group 45, Naval Records Collection of the Office of Naval Records and Library, National Archives, Washington, D.C.

Official Records of the Union and Confederate Navies in the War of the Rebellion (Washington, D.C.: U.S. Navy Department, 1894–1922), series 2, vol. 2, 86.

David M. Sullivan, "Robert M. Ramsey, C.S.M.C.," *Military Images* 11, no. 6 (May–June 1981): 3; David M. Sullivan, "Confederate States Marine Corps Officers' Uniforms: Mobile Naval Station, 1863," *Military Collector & Historian* 50, no. 4 (winter 1998): 175–76.

Ralph W. Donnelly, *The Confederate States Marine Corps: The Rebel Leathernecks* (Shippensburg, Pa.: White Mane Publishing Co., 1989), 241.

Quarterly Returns of Clothing, Camp and Garrison Equipage Issued and Received by Companies A, B, C, and E, C.S. Marine Corps, 1861–1864, Subject file of the C.S. Navy, Subject file O, "Operations of Naval Ships and Fleet Units," file OV, "Miscellaneous," Record Group 45, Naval Records Collection of the Office of Naval Records and Library, National Archives, Washington, D.C.

Ralph W. Donnelly, "More on Confederate Marine Uniforms," *Military Collector & Historian* 31, no. 4 (winter 1979): 170–71; verbal description of the uniform worn by Pvt. Samuel Curtis, CSMC, preserved by his family since 1865, and now in the hands of a descendant.

UNITED STATES MARINES, 1861–65

David M. Sullivan, "The Marine Battalion at Bull Run: Emending the Record," *Leatherneck* (February 2002): 42–49.

Orders issued by John Harris, colonel, commandant, Headquarters, Marine Corps, Washington, D.C., April 27, 1861: "Regulations for the Field Officers of the Corps," Washington, D.C., July 15, 1863, entry 4, "Letters Sent: August 1798–June 1801; March 1804–February 1884," Record Group 127, *Records of the U.S. Marine Corps,* National Archives, Washington, D.C.

Maj. C. G. McCawley, USMC, Maj. George R. Graham, USMC, and 1st Lt. Norval L. Nokes, USMC (members of a Board of Survey) to Col. Jacob Zeilen, Commandant, U.S. Marine Corps, Marine Barracks, Washington, July 20, 1864, entry 42, " Letters Received: 1818–1915," Record Group 127, National Archives.

Regulations for the Uniform and Dress of the Marine Corps of the United States, October 1859, from the Original Text and Drawings in the Quarter Master's Department (Philadelphia: Charles Desilver, 1859).

VETERAN RESERVE CORPS, CORPORAL, 8TH REGIMENT, MARCH 1864

Frederick H. Dyer, *A Compendium of the War of the Rebellion* (New York: Thomas Yoseloff, 1959), 3:1741.

"Quartermaster's Manual of 1864" (never published, but planned for publication by Thomas Publications of Gettysburg, Pa.).

UNION ARMY SURGEON, 1861-65

Regulations for the Army of the United States, 1861 (New York: Harper & Brothers, 1861).

Harold L. Peterson, *The American Sword, 1775–1945* (Philadelphia: Ray Riling Arms Books, 1970).

CONFEDERATE STATES MEDICAL SERVICE

Deering J. Roberts, M.D., C.S. Army surgeon, *Confederate Medical Department,* www. Civilwarhome.com.

Frederick P. Todd, *American Military Equipage* (Providence, R.I.: Company of Military Historians, 1977), 2:493.

Lt. Col. Arthur J. L. Fremantle, *Three Months in the Southern States* (Edinburgh: W. Blackwood, 1863).

PIONEER, ARMY OF THE CUMBERLAND, 1863

National Archives, Record Group 94, entry 12, Letters Received, Adjutant General's Office, 1851.

Letter written by Isaac Raub, copy in Troiani Collection.

William K. Emerson, *Chevrons: An Illustrated History* (Washington, D.C.: Smithsonian Institution Press, 1983).

SERGEANT OF ORDNANCE, 1863

National Archives, Record Group 92, entry 2177, Letters Received by the Philadelphia Depot Quartermaster.

Regulations for the Army of the United States (New York: Harper & Brothers, 1861), article XIV, paragraphs 127–39.

James J. Farley, *Making Arms in the Machine Age: Philadelphia's Frankfort Arsenal, 1816–1870* (University Park, Pa.: Pennsylvania State University Press, 1994).

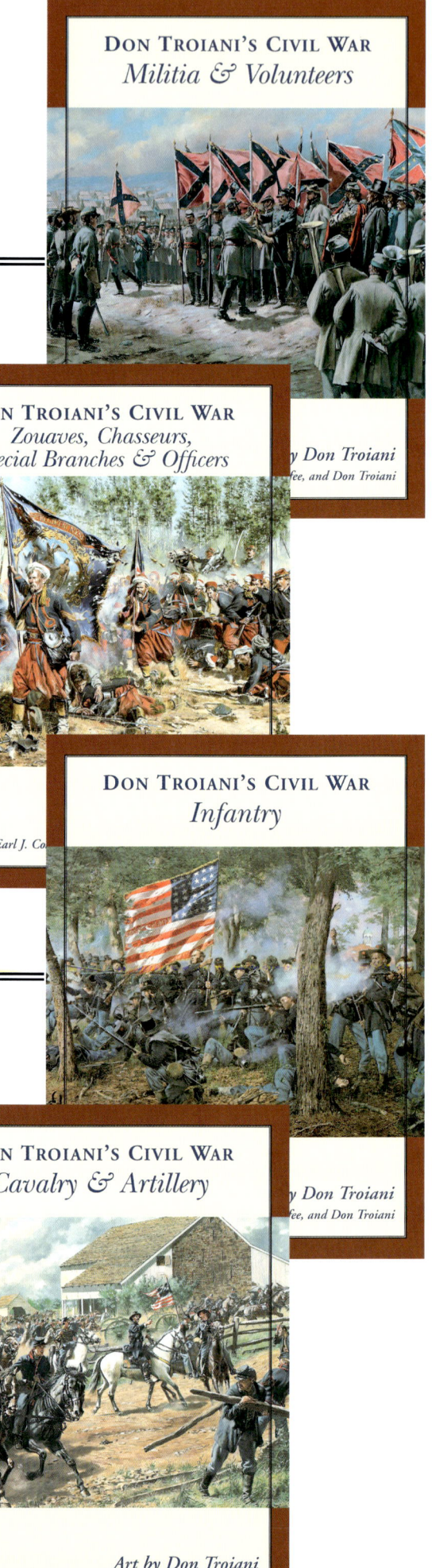